become who you are

VALERIE AIELLO

Created, Designed & Illustrated By Valerie Aiello

© 2023 Goal Party

Name: Aiello, Valerie, author

Title: Become Who You Are

Subjects: Success | Creative Thinking | Optimism | New Thought

**NOT LEGAL, HEALTH OR FINANCIAL ADVICE.
FOR EDUCATIONAL AND INFORMATIONAL PURPOSES ONLY.**

No part of this publication may be reproduced, distributed, or transmitted in any form or by any means, including photocopying, recording, or other electronic or mechanical methods, without prior written permission of the publisher, except in the case of brief quotations embodied in critical reviews and certain other noncommercial uses permitted by copyright law. For permission requests, write to the publisher at the website or by phone 512-814-6579.

ISBN: 978-1-954557-12-3 (Hardcover)

An imprint of Goal Party

Austin, Texas

United States of America

w w w . g o a l p a r t y . c o m

THANK *you*

become WHO you ARE

CHAPTER 1 | **INTRODUCTION** 10

CHAPTER 2 | **FAILURE FATIGUE** 16

CHAPTER 3 | **EVERYONE'S PATH IS DIFFERENT** 28

CHAPTER 4 | **DESIGN YOUR DAY** 36

CHAPTER 5 | **LIST YOUR GOALS** 44

CHAPTER 6 | **BE OPEN TO HOW LIFE UNFOLDS** 52

CHAPTER 7 | **GRATITUDE** 60

CHAPTER 8 | **DON'T FALL ASLEEP WISHING** 66

CHAPTER 9 | **MONETIZE YOU** 72

CHAPTER 10 | **PERSONAL BRAND** 84

become WHO *you* ARE

CHAPTER 11 | IS SOCIAL MEDIA IMPORTANT?   96

CHAPTER 12 | BROADCAST YOU   106

CHAPTER 13 | CUSTOMERS, FANS & FRIENDS   118

CHAPTER 14 | SELF-AWARENESS   130

CHAPTER 15 | INSPIRE JUST ONE PERSON   140

CHAPTER 16 | REVERSE ENGINEER YOUR GOALS   146

CHAPTER 17 | YOU'VE ALREADY MADE IT   152

CHAPTER 18 | LIFESTYLE FREEDOM   158

CHAPTER 19 | INSPIRE YOURSELF   168

CHAPTER 20 | HOW TO PLAY GUITAR   176

Why me? I am not a life-coach. I am not a teacher. I am not a philosopher. I am not a therapist. I am not a millionaire. I am not famous. I do not have a social media following to speak of. I have not overcome some major tragedy, pulling myself out of some hell. I am just a person that hasn't had a hit yet. One could even say, "You are not successful enough. Why on earth would you write a book?" Given the right moment of an insecure downward spiral, I just might hunch my shoulders and sneak off to cry myself a river. Just like any other normal person that doesn't have the perfect image of exactly what they imagine to be standing in front of them in the mirror, I am deciding to show up and share with you here. Here I am. Here you are (hopefully) reading this book that somehow magically got into your hands.

Hello there. How's it going? I am Valerie Aiello, and I would like to welcome you to my book. My first book with my name on it as the author. Will it suck? Probably. Will anyone besides my friends and family receiving this book as a gift, open this book? Doubtful. Honestly, I do not know exactly what will happen after this book hits the street. I am 100% certain that I will regret publishing this, feel super embarrassed, and probably look back in fear that I ever put my thoughts down on paper for the entire world to read. Publishing this is very scary and super embarrassing.

Regardless of the outcome, I have this super positive energy pulling me to create this book. I am jumping into the game. I'm standing here in front of the unknown with the tiniest of spotlights on me giving you my mind and heart.

I haven't accomplished all the things. I do not have everything that I want. I have felt like crap for years wondering when is something good going to happen to me? Where are my millions? No one cares about what I am doing. I feel like I am on an island. Um...mic check, is this thing on? I have felt so underrated, underutilized, underachieving...blah, blah, blah. Doubt inevitably enters the mind a little everyday and I start to believe that maybe I am not as much of a genius as I think I am. However, I got over it, got it together, and understood one simple thing; I do have something valuable to add to the world today even if I never change. I can make a product meaningful to share, and the success of it has nothing to do with sales or how much money it produces. The success of it is just based on the fun it is to make, and the hopes of one person being inspired to make their own thing they have been afraid to put out in the world today.

Some questions you might have before we get started. What the heck is this book about? Is this self-help dribble? Maybe. Is this a religious book? I don't think so. Is this witchcraft? Not that I know of. Is this a spiritual book? That is not my intention. Is this a quantum physics book? I wish. I'm not sure exactly how this fits into any specific subject, but the label that I feel most comfortable slapping on this is "Positive Thinking." I feel like positive thinking has always been a big part of my soul. Now, I understand that positive thinking is a real tangible thing that I can use to trampoline myself to more happiness, and even more awesome experiences.

What I am saying here is not anything that hasn't been said before by a ton of different people throughout history. I am unique, but the concepts here are as old as time. I'm here to give my interpretation of positive thinking. This book is not meant to be psychological advice, financial advice, or a replacement for therapy. You are responsible for your own choices, actions, and results for becoming who you are. The most important thing I want you to know is that you can start right now being any version of yourself that you can dream up.

So, here I am. For the people out there that may think I am totally making a fool out of myself for putting my heart on my sleeve for everyone to read, bring it! Bad reviews and hate comments can come flooding in. I will be okay. I'll be over here looking on the bright side!

If by some small chance I could be the one to introduce positive thinking to someone in a new way that brings them a mindset shift toward success, that would be amazing. If this book can be the catalyst to change someone's life for the better, I am all for it!

Let's go!

Let's start with the bad news. The ups and downs of trying to become successful doing exactly what you want to do can be painful. Do not get paranoid, but it can feel like people are judging you. It hurts to want something that isn't happening. It can hurt to not be able to buy nice gifts for people, or go out with everyone to fancy dinners, or just simply do something at the professional level you crave and feel ready for.

The truth is: failure is necessary to the learning process. On the brightside, feeling like crap is there to help you. Your feelings become your goals. I know, that sounds ambiguous. What I mean is, when you experience something painful it's an indicator that you need to make a shift. On the flipside when you experience something exciting, that's an indicator your goals are unfolding as you hoped. Maybe a shift comes from within your mind, maybe a shift comes from learning a valuable lesson the hard way, and maybe a shift comes from gaining a new skill. You may need to cut things from your life, evaluate relationships, current jobs, or forgo something that is really hard to live without at the moment. Your feelings are going to spark your brain to create a new solution for you that will bring you closer to your goals. No one knows the outcome of failure when it happens. But, the one thing I can say with 100% certainty is that failure is a gift. It's just a part of the process. However, there is something that happens when you are building something and focusing on the long game: Failure fatigue, a term I use to describe not reaching your desired success for years. Dare I say decades. Here are ten questions to ask yourself if you are experiencing failure fatigue.

"Am I being impatient?" - Does this dream take some people a lifetime to achieve? Are you getting all bent out of shape, because you are 3 years in with no results? You've got to suck it up. Dust the dirt off from your pride. Wipe the tears from your eye, and keep working at it. This is a long game. You are where you are. Just be proud of yourself now, and keep getting better everyday. Take a break if you are in pain and just simply need one. It's possible you need to double down on the amount of time you put in, or it just simply takes more time than you could ever imagine. Change your mindset to see the long periods of time without provable success in a new light to have more fun. Reevaluate what you envision your everyday life should look like. It is possible you have the wrong idea of what success looks like. Even if you are not proud of yourself, maybe someone with a similar dream would look at your life in envy, because you actually have come a long way building towards your goal. You are in control of how you react to your experience, and there are no rules when it comes to your happiness. Being patient and proud of yourself today without needing some magical imaginary "finish line" proof of success is a huge help for my failure fatigue.

"Do I have unrealistic expectations?" - If you are doing something new, you may not actually know how to do it yet. It could take years of apprenticeship, research, practicing, mentor advice, or failures to make your specific goal happen. You may not know how long some people have to work to achieve success. What helps me is researching biographies of successful people that had public failures to see how they pulled themselves out of the hard times. Also, I pick people to research that seemingly had success overnight. Once you dive into their story, you may find out that they started working a full 10 years before they even had one ounce of success.

"Am I an ungrateful jerk?" - What have you accomplished so far? I bet there are a million people that would happily trade places with you right now. You may have come farther along in your success than you think.

That realization happened to me a few times. During one of my many failure fatigue moments, I came to my senses after feeling not successful enough for about 5 years of consistently working on a business without much profitability. I finally got it into my head that I was being really ungrateful. My life is actually freaking easy. People suffer everyday going to jobs they hate for decades, and still not achieving everything they want out of life, living paycheck to paycheck. I wasn't doing that. I had obtained the skills and the confidence to casually pick and choose big and small client gigs as an Art Director to work on as I needed. I was working remotely from any location I wanted to be. I created a situation for myself that gave me tons of free time to create and work on my goals. I didn't have what a normal person would consider success, or more importantly, what I consider to be success for myself. Being the best Art Director in the world was not a top priority for me. If a job was going to be a part of my life, choosing to work with design sounded fun to me. I did not have the bank account of my dreams. I did not have all the experiences of my dreams. However, because of the skills I have built up over time, I did have unconventional relaxing work freedom to create anything I could dream up daily. That is something to be proud of.

While you're sitting there feeling sorry for yourself, which is very easy for probably everyone, try to look on the brightside. There are probably tons of people that would love to trade places with you right this very moment. Get a grip dude, and stop feeling sorry for yourself.

"Did I do something wrong?" - No one is perfect. You have heard that a million times before. Sure, you probably did do something wrong, but the good news is that there is always a solution. When you are feeling guilty, or just going through the same miserable experiences over and over with the same or different people, it is important to stop and investigate. Ask yourself, "do I need to apologize? Do I need to change?" Take responsibility. Take opportunities to learn and make changes for the better. While experiencing these hard situations it is very hard to look in the mirror to figure out how to have a positive outcome with the same mind that created the problem. Also remember, you are not on an island, sometimes asking for help hashing out problems is the best thing you can do. Teach yourself how to forgive, apologize, and improve with grace. Do whatever you need to do to learn from mistakes, and try your best to bring kindness, love and education to the situation.

"It's not my fault" - Sure, tragedies happen, Some things knock you back 1000 feet, and there is no way you could have ever seen it coming. It is so annoying when it is not your fault. I don't even want to say it...but ask yourself how you find the teachable moment from tragedy and build yourself up stronger? Being a human on this planet is so amazing, but there is some risk to the experience. You can stay inside all day alone, never interacting with people, and try to ensure every possibility to avoid pain. There is a silver lining in a bad situation, investigate your heart and mind. Ask for help. There is no right answer for how you find your brightside. There is also no time limit to have everything figured out. Positive thinking is sitting there waiting for you to hold your hand to start figuring things out.

"Do I need to pivot?" - Patience is very important when building a unique life and business, becoming who you are. I am a very patient person naturally, but even I probably wait too long to notice when the time has come to make some changes. When is pivoting necessary? When success is taking forever It might seem from the outside looking in that you are a crazy person with no real goals or integrity to finish what you have started. But, when the writing's on the wall that something is not going to work, and no amount of time or effort is going to make it work for you, it is time to pivot. That doesn't mean your previous plan was a bad plan. There could be a million reasons why a goal is not panning out for you. I've noticed that people feel ashamed to pivot on ideas.

Sometimes people announce to the world their brand new sparkling project, just to leave it on the side of the road a few months later. You hope no one will notice. Then you go to parties, and people you never even told about your project ask you how your project is going. Then you remember, oh yeah, I blasted all over every social media platform for months what hopeful plans were set. Then you are left wishing you had a mind-erasing machine to take it all back. If you are embarrassed about pivoting, don't be. People don't really care for the most part, they want you to be happy. You might be the type of person that needs to keep things under wraps until it's a reality. You might be a person that telling the entire world exactly what you are doing gives you motivation to complete something hard. Everyone is different, just don't feel guilty.

Sometimes you need to ask yourself if you actually want to do the dream that you had in mind. I had a friend in high school who was captain of the debate team. They worked everyday at their maximum potential to get into a good college, then got into the best law school they could get into. That's over a decade of extreme hard work to prepare for a dream. Then once they started working as a real lawyer, they completely hated it. I think maybe it took a year, then they pivoted to a completely different dream. I guess someone could say so much of their time was wasted just to quit after all that effort. I say, no way! Are you kidding me! Think of how much knowledge one gains from a decade of studying and accomplishing something. Who cares how long you do something professionally if you learn stuff. Keep growing, learning and experiencing. Once you achieve one goal, it could turn out to be something that you really are not into. Maybe the knowledge gained in the process of learning that something is not for you is actually the perfect thing you need to go onto the next step. Pivot without fear!

"Do I need help to achieve my goals?" - No one is good at everything. You may need a team. You may need just one more person to achieve success, but ultimately you may just need help. Stop feeling sorry for yourself and look for solutions that work for you. Sometimes you need to take tasks off your plate that are painfully boring to you. That awful task could be a future partner's most thrilling task ever. Team up with someone. Outsource something. Hire someone. There are a million ways you can try out getting help that works for you with little risk. Would you rather have 100% of zero profits, or 1% of a piece of something actually successful? If you are unhappy with your result, and you are feeling like a failure, try getting some help.

"Is my intuition broken?" - Failure fatigue can come in different forms. Things could be perfect from the outside looking in, and you still feel a nagging tinge of unfulfillment. Come up with a plan to switch it up. There could be something much more exciting just around the corner if you just pay attention to how you really feel.

Do you just absolutely love what you do, but no one seems to care? Sure, your intuition on approach could be wrong, but keep trying different ways to make it happen. The right place at the right time could be just around the corner. Your intuition is guiding you, keep investigating and executing. There is at least 1% chance things could unfold for you perfectly. There is a 100% chance nothing happens if you give up. You do not have dreams to suffer never achieving them. Sure, things may not happen on your timeline, you may feel like a loser, but keep doing the work to find your own way to become who you are.

"Do I need a break?" - There are 12-year-old millionaire entrepreneurs "crushing it" right now with high dollar speaking gigs. There are 70 year-olds starting their modeling careers right now. Pivoting doesn't have to be the answer if you are in pain having failure fatigue. Maybe taking a break and putting a project or business on the back-burner is a perfectly healthy thing to do. I often struggle with this question myself. If fate exists, can you manifest destiny? How important is effort? I haven't found a clear answer. I think the answer could be, just work on being the best you can be. No one is going to yell at you if you need to put everything on hold for a year. Focus on another goal. Become a housesitter on a tropical island. Decide to wait tables for a few months to build up a nest egg. Come back to a goal refreshed, stronger, and maybe with a new perspective. There are no rules! Remember, this is a long game. There is no harm in taking a timeout.

"Is perfectionism holding me back?" - I, unfortunately, do not have this problem. If I am interested in something, I like to do the best I can at that moment, create it, and put it out for the world to see. I do not always like to wait to be perfect at something just to try it. For some people, that sounds like a nightmare. I admire people that take things to the next-level for every project they create. I'm jealous of people that can make sure every single element is created in total perfection, then release it to the world. However, if perfection is a crutch stopping you from actually doing your thing, then it might be holding you back. Some people say, "perfection is just procrastination in disguise."

Everyone starts somewhere. We all suck at the beginning. You probably suck right now at something you want to try. I am pretty sure I suck right now at writing books, but here I am. Even amazing people suck sometimes, but they find the courage inside to start, suck, and improve.

Now, turn off that sad bastard music. Get out of here, and go for it!

So, do you want to be a scuba diving instructor / lawyer / pastry chef? Do you want to be a CEO / professional pottery maker / comedian? Do you want to be an accountant / filmmaker / helicopter pilot / commercial songwriting music producer? What do you want to be? It doesn't matter. You can be anything you want. You do not have to choose one. Being a multi-hyphenated professional is okay. It might take you longer than average to achieve it all. Your talent might max out at being the most average skill level of the careers you choose, but you can still choose to do it. You have a lifetime to try new things, build new skills and become who you are.

Some people are lucky enough to have just one dream job, and they know in their heart that they will always want to do that one thing. That is probably an amazing feeling and experience to just build one career for an entire life. It is no one's place to say if that is an easier path or not. It could be easier by focusing all your efforts on one goal. However, that one goal could be massively difficult with decades of education. That is one path to choose toward success. However, many people are multi-passionate. That is another path to choose for building a successful life.

Lately, there seems to be this obsession to "be your own boss;" and to "quit your day job." There is a lot of pain associated with daily job drudgery and doing something you hate to do. It is a great thing to lift people up, to inspire them to do what they love, to help them realize they can build up their skills and their confidence to never have to work a job that sucks. I am absolutely against feeling drudgery when it comes to spending 40 hours or more weekly doing something that brings zero value other than a paycheck. On the other hand, what if you love your "day job?" What if that day job is exactly the perfectly fun thing that makes your life more fulfilling? What if you actually need that day job to learn the skills needed to achieve more dreams in a perfectly balanced schedule of happiness. What if bartending brings you interesting conversations, money, friendships and joy? What if working minimum wage at a museum brings you closer to culture, gives you time to study art history, and relaxation. What if going to make the donuts at 3 a.m awakens your creativity? What if having an easy side-hustle paycheck awakens your confidence and relaxation to do something that you really want to try?

If you have just one goal or a multitude of skills, talents, and dreams to work with, you can make your own schedule. You can have simultaneous professional careers, or just one thing you do everyday for the rest of your life. Everyone's path is different.

Personally, I am a mega-multitasker, and I love to have several plates spinning in the air that interest me. I have literal suitcases in my closets jammed-packed with papers of ideas, business plans, and products developed that do not exist yet. I would love to try them all. I have hundreds of ideas every week. They are not all good ones, but I keep thinking and building new ideas. Some ideas I am currently working on, some are on back-burners for later dates, and some I should probably just keep in that closet. However, I've boiled them all down to one chief aim, and I have decided I am a professional Product Developer. That's what I do all day long, everyday. I just work on whatever product that I feel as if the time has come to give it a try.

I like having lots of options, and lots of projects going at the same time by myself or with different teams. It has taken me some time to finally get focused enough and brave enough to say, "I do not take client work" or have a "day job." I only work on my own products and projects. My way is probably not the right way, but I share with you to let you know that it is possible to have all your time to yourself if that is what you want. I am just a normal person, and I love it that I am here. I feel like I'm on the right path, but who knows, something could magically fall in my lap that could change everything. The world could change, I could change, and I would be open to it. My path is as unique as yours, and I hope you are excited everyday to build your own path.

There is one little bummer we cannot forget when deciding how to build a dream life, and that is paying dues. Some people can work a job all day, then come home and work on another business. Some people work at a corporate job for twenty years; getting the highest level professional skills they can get until the day they decide to start their own business. Some people need to work those 12-hour-day, 6-days-a-week grueling jobs for a decade just to know exactly how a company runs well. Sometimes, the only way to be as successful as a business owner for yourself is to put in the years of learning. It's called paying dues. Paying your dues is totally worth it when you are becoming who you are. Some dues are fun. Some dues are painful. Some are just about going through the motions. Whatever your path is will determine what your dues are and how long you have to do them. Maybe it's just something you have to do forever. Maybe what seems like a nightmare to some, might be exhilarating for you.

Every situation for every person unfolds differently. Punching a time clock is soul-sucking for some, and invigorating for others. There are people that show up to jobs everyday that have a personal entrepreneur business as well. Don't feel like you have to fit into any mold to become who you are. You could go to college or not go to college. You could get a salary. You could just take client gigs. You could collect rent checks as income, or walk to the mailbox once a month for a royalty check. There are a million ways to solve the problem of having security, happiness, and freedom.

NOTES

Let's talk about something actionable to help solve the occasional failure fatigue, and the spiraling out of focus to get distracted from goals. I design my day. What does that mean? Simply put, I have a small daily lifestyle to-do list of actions that never change. If I accomplish these things daily, it makes me feel that I am living my dream life doing exactly what I want to be doing. That doesn't mean that I pretend everything is perfect, but at the very least that I am slowly working towards something that I want for my future. This helps me remove distractions or tasks that aren't helping me design my day, and effortlessly guides me to make sure I am actually doing the things that I love to do daily.

If I move forward a little bit everyday to become who I am, I feel proud of myself. This comforts me to lose the guilt of not getting everything done. This supports me to give myself grace for not being perfect. If I keep focused on this short lifestyle to-do list, I know I have made some progress. Even if that progress was just a little tiny bit of improvement. Simply "trying" does mean something when you have giant impossible goals that you know only can be achieved with time and effort. I probably spent ten years straight of stressing myself out every single night, because "everything" was not done. I felt miserable not feeling as successful as I thought I should be. Designing my day with a short lifestyle daily to-do list helped me lower my stress substantially!

Your short daily lifestyle to-do list may look very different. Just as an example, I am going to share with you mine. I have boiled down my day to focus on achieving five main tasks daily to strive for the feeling of having a valuable day.

1. CREATE ONE PRODUCT - If I have to give myself one title to describe what I do, it is Product Developer. I know that doesn't mean much when you don't work for a fancy company and just work for yourself, but that is what I feel encapsulates it. I don't put many rules on what I should be doing exactly everyday, but making sure I am taking my ideas and constructing it into something real to share with the world is my aim. What is a product? Well, for me, it could be a song, a book, artwork, a video game, a technology solution, a real estate deal, the options are probably ridiculously endless. My favorite type of product to produce is something I can work on once, and then sell repeatedly collecting a royalty from a sale. When I am working on this one task daily, it is extremely important to complete projects and have them actually exist to be published for the marketplace. However, it's not the most important act. Continuously working to complete things is good enough for me to feel accomplished. My ultimate goal is to make valuable products for people to enjoy, and hopefully make them feel cooler. So, I spend every day getting better and better at building products.

2. EXECUTE ONE MARKETING GOAL - I do not get crazy stressed about this. I do what I can. Usually, I pick the most fun idea to work on, and go for it. This might include creating an ad, a social media post, a photoshoot, writing an article, submitting press releases, or creating new digital marketing materials. Just whatever happens, happens. I try to find a happy medium between creating awareness for one of my products, and fashioning something that I feel is educational, valuable or simply heartfelt to share with the world.

3. CREATE ONE PODCAST EPISODE - This is a future goal that I slowly work on every week. Being able to communicate ideas over the internet does not come naturally for most. I

would say it is an uncomfortable task for me to grab a microphone, turn on the camera, and start talking to the world. Nevertheless, my intuition tells me that it is a skill that I need for the future. My show is named, "Idea Diary." I call it a business lifestyle podcast, because I do not technically have a specific focus for the show just yet. Currently my goal is to practice casually communicating my business experiences in a professional way. Even though it is a scary undertaking, it does feel fun to produce a podcast, and I have a strong urge to comply with my instinct to learn this skill. After every episode is published, I feel more accomplished. Having a successful podcast is a ten year goal for me. Whatever the outcome of the success level of the podcast is irrelevant to me. The achievement here is to get technically better at producing an interesting valuable show; and communicating adequately with the world.

4. WORKOUT - Sometimes I get super organized by making sure I get outside to walk and listen to music everyday, and sometimes I fail to make it happen. It's a daily goal nevertheless.

5. CLEAN - Having a zero-clutter space to work is mandatory for me to keep my brain at a high capacity of function. Making sure everything has a place really helps my business mind expand. That's not to say that being neat is mandatory for everyone to feel comfortable and functional. I cannot say my house is always ready for surprise visitors at any moment, but that is my goal. I strive to have a place for everything, no junk drawers, and space to create.

I follow the strategies that teach you to stop and spend 15- 30 minutes a day to clean something in your house by rotating tasks. The idea is you never have to spend an entire day cleaning an entire house. This method does help me feel consistently clean and decluttered. Although, I do not look around and feel like everything is perfect. I do have a clear vision of what my ultimate live/work space would feel and look like, and I would like to think that I get closer to that goal everyday.

So, that is my daily lifestyle short to-do list. Your list may have more or less responsibilities based on what will make you feel accomplished and relaxed after the day is done. Again, this doesn't mean you have to do it like me. Design your day so it feels exciting and authentic to you. Add new tasks, take away old tasks that aren't bringing you joy, change your mind, take your time figuring out what is really right for you. Just try to not go to bed without doing anything that you actually want to be doing with your life to become who you are.

It took me a long time to finally remove all the day-to-day distractions that were not getting me closer to my goals. Most of my days now feel very similar with a ton of time and space to create, which is what I need. You may require something totally different to function at your highest level. Hustle culture can be great for achieving big chunks of goals at certain times of life. It can feel exciting to have a million things going on all at once, but I prefer a slow day to categorically decide what is most meaningful for me to work on.

I also have different types of dream routines that I like to imagine as possible experiences I want to have. Organizing dream mornings, dream evenings, dream workdays, dream weekends is something I may pause to journal about if I feel overwhelmed. Daydreaming to understand the big picture of how I want to exist daily helps me organize my reality. This is not magic. Taking myself seriously and writing down exactly how I imagine my dream lifestyle is relaxing. Even if I am not living my dream routines at the current moment, being focused with clarity helps me establish what I need to do to get there. It does take some time and discipline to know yourself, and to organize your perfect high-function days, perfect lazy days, perfect family days and friend days.

GUIDED JOURNAL IDEA - Take a moment to journal about your unique ultimate perfect moments of the day. Design some busy mornings, and some slow mornings. Design some highly productive days, and some lazy days. Design different locations, repetitive tasks, or different daily experiences you would love to accomplish regularly.

I break down daily scenarios by dream mornings, dream afternoons, dream evenings, dream vacations, and dream conferences. I will grab my diary, and journal my dream routines if I am feeling constantly distracted, not producing much, or totally out of alignment with how relaxed and organized that I want to feel daily. The important thing is to validate your ideas and be self-assured that you are aware that you can plan ahead, meet your expectations, and experience life with intention eventually; even if it's not today.

There are a ton of people that do whatever they want everyday. It doesn't take fame or a million dollars. You can be one of those people too if you plan and work towards it.

Some people might say that a list of goals is just a wish list of things that you are never going to do. Sure, you may never actually achieve all your goals, but the magic of writing them down for organizing your mind is undeniable. I believe that getting your goals down on paper does actually help manifest those goals into your reality. I would not say that writing down goals helps to make things happen faster, easier, or any other "get rich quick" kind of scheme someone might sell you. However, there is so much proof out there that writing things down does help people achieve more. There has got to be some science behind it. I do not know what that science is, but you could spend hours watching videos on the topic of the science of writing things down.

Taking yourself seriously and writing down and organizing all your hopes and dreams is worth the effort to see how things unfold. Some of your goals might be daily goals, and some of your goals might be accomplishments that take decades to achieve. Goals might be impossible feats that you achieve without even knowing how it happened. Some goals might be surprisingly awful to experience, so pick out new goals. Taking goals off your plate that don't excite you anymore is just as important as not giving up on dreams. Not to mention, you will also add numerous goals to your list as you add new skills, experience, and knowledge to your repertoire.

There are three things that I find important when it comes to listing my goals: ONE, have your goals easy to access, TWO, get creative with communicating your goals, and THREE, list short term goals and long term goals often.

Having a goal list on me at all times helps keep my overall main intentions in life on the front of my mind at all times. Being able to look at goals at any moment is like a little lightning bolt of concentrated energy going right into your conscience and subconscious mind. This helps keep ambition on track.

I love to have my goals on one sheet of paper. I will list daily goals then monthly goals, and keep writing down until I get a big picture of what I would like to be doing decades from now. Doing this type of journaling is not something I do everyday. It is something I do every New Year's Eve, whenever something goes horribly wrong to readjust, or when I am feeling out of alignment with my target goals.

Never forget… do take into consideration that you may change your mind. Sometimes you think, if I only accomplished "that thing" then I will feel successful. Then you achieve "that thing" and you don't feel any different. So you pile on more "things" to achieve, and you still do not feel accomplished. Reaching goals can spiral into a totally different conversation about happiness. The important thing about goals is to have them, start going for them even if they seem impossible, and not be afraid to change your mind if you feel like it.

Next, get creative with how you keep your goal list organized.

Make your list in the way that feels most fun and valuable for you. Keep post-its on a fridge, carry around a luxury daily planner with a calligraphy pen, or have it typed up digitally in a notes application on your phone. Everyone's brain works differently, and the possibilities of creatively organizing goals that become realized are endless.

I am an illustrator, so I like to draw my goals. I make little clip art images that represent all the things I want to achieve. I make one digital collage image that I keep on my phone. I do this once a year. Every new year, it is always interesting to see which goals actually happened, which goals I have decided to put on the back-burner, which goals I changed my mind about, and the new ideas that I add to my goal collage after one year.

Your goals could be tattoos on your arm, or one sentence you keep on your bedside to read over and over again, or an entire fictional novel you've written about your dream life. Use your unique skills to really enjoy designing your dream life.

I heard someone suggest that your living space could be a 3D manifestation board. This sounded like a very creative way to keep goals on the forefront of the mind, as well as, continuously communicating with your subconscious mind. I have been working on creating and displaying paintings that represent future dream accomplishments. Plus, giving all my furniture and home decor significant special thoughtful meanings for my gratitude and goals. Decorating is not one of my greatest talents, but designing a space with lots of hopeful future dreams signification, personality, and zero clutter is definitely on my goal list. It might take some time for me to actually deliberately design every angle of a living space, but I can see the value in creating it. I am thoughtfully consciously working on it!

Lastly, listing short term and long term goals regularly is something that I love to do. This will mean something different for everyone, depending on how busy your life is and how much is on your list. Personally, I keep my daily goals as minimal as possible. I hate to be unnecessarily busy. I also hate to get distracted by things that I do not want to do, but sometimes those go on the short list. This takes some planning to be able to casually function while actually achieving things slowly. It would be awesome to get things done faster, but it is a thoughtful process to balance out your dream schedule.

With the long term goals, I have a one sheet spread in a journal that I keep on the bookshelf for grabbing when it feels like it is time to revisit and organize my long term goals. When I don't feel like journaling, I just look at my illustrated goal collage JPEG that I keep on my phone to go over at any moment.

GUIDED JOURNAL IDEA - Sit down and make decisions of what you want to happen in your life, then list your goals. Keep this list in a place that is easy to revisit in the best method for your skill style.

Daily Goals

Monthly Goals

Yearly Goals

5 year Goals

10 year Goals

Hopefully, you have a peaceful, easy feeling to design your unique life path, with all your goals and dream routines all laid out. And of course, you know that you are going to win some and lose some. You know that success can possibly take forever, and you may have nothing to show for all your hard work for months or even years. The daily experience of becoming who you are must be what is important to achieving your plans, and being simply patient with yourself as you work is key. Now, be open to how things unfold.

Have a plan, but let go of your ideas of how you imagine things are supposed to happen. Sure, your plan might be perfect, but you could be thinking small and not even know it. Something bigger, brighter, and more fascinating could unfold while you are sitting there being furious that things aren't going your way.

Good and bad things happen for you. It is never really known what is coming up around the corner. When things go wrong, take a minute. Cry about it, but then put on that positive thinking cap and look on the bright side. This is something I have learned with age, but when crap hits the fan or when success is taking forever, instead of spiraling into a pity party, I stop and ask myself "What am I supposed to be learning from this moment?" What are the awesome possibilities that could unfold now that there is new information. What moves can I make? What can I try now or change to achieve more greatness or simply have more fun right now?

If you want different results than you are getting, try something new. It might be time to pivot to a new idea. It also might be time to put a goal on the backburner for a while. Trying to force a good idea at the wrong time is not always the best strategy. Your job is not to plan every single moment of your life, but to rather practice, learn, test, try, give, live, take chances, and build your desires into reality by getting started. There is only so much in your control. Dream big, and be open.

I'm not saying to not plan. There is a balance between giving up, taking breaks, and just moving forward with no results. Plan your heart out, or go with the flow. Everyone is going to get through their journey differently. Some people might plan every moment of the day. Some people might hit a highway to hitchhike anywhere, not knowing what comes from hour to hour without a dime to their name. The unknown is irrelevant in both situations. Your learning process, imagination, and feelings, are all going to affect the outcomes of your decision-making from moment to moment. You never know how you might feel tomorrow, so have your best day ever today.

I have talked about pivoting ideas. I have talked about pulling oneself out of failure fatigue, and I have talked about taking a break, but what happens when you want to stop and give up?

You will have to know inside your heart what the right thing to do is. People give up on dreams at all ages, and people have unexpected success at all ages. I think the main question you need to ask yourself is, would you like to die knowing that you are the person that never gave up on that goal, or do you feel at peace knowing you moved on?

One time, I went on a winter break from a gift shop that I opened and ran by myself. I traveled after the holiday shopping season to go hunting for new products, and I simply needed a change of pace. I was in the habit of doing whatever I wanted to do from the moment I woke up until the moment I fell asleep. Admittedly, opening my own gift shop was fun, but it was sort of cramping my style, having to be in the same place everyday to run a store.

When I went on that break, I never thought in a million years that I would come home just to close up that shop for good. However, during that break I assessed the situation, and came up with a more fulfilling and profitable plan for myself. Was the original plan bad? Not necessarily. Did I waste a year of time being open and working everyday in a gift shop? Not at all! I just decided that I had learned all the valuable lessons I could reasonably learn from the experience at that time, and I made a new choice. No big whoop. Having to explain to everyone that asked how the gift shop was doing over and over was a little annoying, but not as annoying as doing something I really didn't want to do everyday. I absolutely loved the experience, and I was very happy I had the business instincts to get out as soon as my intuition said it was time to move on to bigger dreams.

When deciding to give up on something you have changed your mind about, ask yourself a few questions: Did you go down every path? Did you try every idea? If you feel satisfied with a new decision, then it's totally an option for everyone to throw in the towel sometimes. Everyone has quit a job in their career path that they prayed hard to get in the beginning. Sometimes, it's time to go.

Just please always consider that everyone is given dreams not because you meant to live in torture by never achiving them, but because you possess all the talent inside to fulfill those dreams. Try, try, try, and try again. Never give up if you really want it.

NOTES

CHAPTER 7 | GRATITUDE

I know. I know. Gratitude… annoying! You are probably thinking, give me a break. That is just more 2006 self-help guru law of attraction repetitive nonsense that doesn't work. Well, you are reading a positive thinking book, so I'm pretty sure you can guess what I am going to say. Stop and find something to be grateful for. Start with one thing, and I bet you can keep listing 100 things before you have to stop listing. We live in an amazing time in history. Some people have more than others, but ultimately almost anything is possible for almost everyone. A person can create one thing, and humans across the entire globe could take notice in a matter of seconds. It is just amazing.

If you stop and look around at your life and surroundings, do you think about how happy you are or think about how everything around you is just a complete disaster? There is a common theory that everything bad that happens in someone's life is their own fault. I do not subscribe to that theory, but I do feel like bad things can happen for a reason that can make life more complete. I believe there is a brightside to all tragedy, misfortune, and hardship if we look for it.

When it comes to gratitude, it is just human to take things for granted. You could feel grateful all day long, and forget to consciously acknowledge it. Creating little moments to remind myself to be grateful for big and small things within my everyday habits works for me. For example, before I am about to sit at my computer to work, I like to grab a coffee and light a candle for gratitude and concentration. Something about this little ritual gets me excited to block out the next few hours just to do something as simple as thinking. When the work is done, I blow out the candle, close my computer, and remember to say thank you for my brain and the opportunity to create today.

Sometimes negative self-talk does creep into the brain. You could have full days of just hating everything around you for seemingly no reason at all. Maybe scrolling through social media spun you into a frenzy of self-pity, because all the seemingly perfect lives feel miles ahead of your success path. I have a tip for that! Just love yourself today, even if you never change.

If you have lived in the same tiny room forever that you hate. If you have worn the same clothes forever. If you never lose weight. If you never become any more successful than you are right now, love yourself today even if you never change. Everyone has different unique obstacles, and sometimes professional help is needed to solve them. Some problems are bigger than anyone can solve alone, so asking for help from professionals and doctors can help build beneficial results. I have come to embrace that finding solutions to problems is what makes me smarter, prosperous, and more me. Being content with how life is today is a peaceful feeling. If you never experience one more moment of success, are you not worth loving? Of course you are. You are still alive! The grass is still green. The sky's still blue. It is still fun to meet up with someone who understands you, and talk for hours. There are a million things to be grateful for beyond what you feel bad about in your head. It would be impossible for nothing good to ever happen to you for the rest of your life. On hopeless days, try to appreciate where you came from and who you are today. Sometimes your basic everyday malaise will feel brighter and easier when you stop yourself to appreciate today.

I know that feeling gratitude when everything sucks today feels impossible. Here is one idea to help bring yourself up to a higher vibe: Give your greatest talent to someone that might need it. You might believe you have nothing to give, but I promise you have something unique to give to someone that needs it. It doesn't need to be money, time, or even physical items. You could write a nice biography for a friend's business. You could record a 20-second original bumper song for a podcast you love, because you notice they don't have an intro song. You could bake some cookies, and visit with an elderly neighbor. You have something to give, even if it's just a phone call, a new idea, or a smile.

It is great to be happy with how things are today, but try not to fall asleep wishing you were doing something else with your life every night.

Maybe your life is hectic. Maybe your life is easy. Maybe you have everything you could ever want. Maybe you don't have two sticks to rub together. Whatever your situation is, don't fall asleep wishing you were doing something else.

Make your list of goals, and pick something to start. Put down this book, and start to become who you are right now. Take that first step to make every dream you have a reality. It doesn't have to all happen overnight for you to feel accomplished. You don't have to "fake it until you make it" as some people might say. No one starts at a professional level attempting anything. Start at a beginner level. You can be anything you want today. A painter, a writer, an actor, a designer, a builder. There is a "day one" for every career. Even a super unique career that no one's ever heard of in the history of the world. Yes, even that crazy idea you have, there is a "day one."

There is no need to ask for permission. Give yourself permission. Do not let fear of failure stop you before you even get started. Do not worry about what people might say. Do not worry about the millions of reasons you have built up in your head why you can't do what you want to do today. Once you get started, you are going to learn all the pitfalls and power moves you will decide to do as you construct your plan. When you are going to sleep tonight, just lay your head down knowing you are what you want to be today. One thing I like to do at night is to make an evening to-do list for what I would like to accomplish the following day. I call this my "Goal Night" list. Sometimes this list is actually small errands that I need to get done, and sometimes I write out big impossible tasks to achieve. I feel like this relaxes me to build a little plan of attack for tomorrow in my head. This evening task also confirms with my subconscious mind all my pipe dream aspirations while I am drifting off to sleep. Does this actually do anything to achieve more goals? Who knows, but I know I feel more organized and accomplished when I end the day knowing exactly what I want to achieve tomorrow.

When you fall asleep with the intention to be exactly who you want to be tomorrow, and do exactly what you want to do, there is not a more powerful feeling. When you wake up everyday moving forward, watching how everything unfolds is going to be awesome to watch. Consciously taking your desires seriously daily, and being open to how things unfold is impressive if you can do it. This is where you may fight the failure fatigue, learn how to intuitively pivot, take breaks, and figure out how to do some of the tedious tasks without feeling drudgery.

But today, you aren't going to worry about that. Today you are at day one or day ten thousand of becoming who you are. This life architecture is something that you probably never retire from, so enjoying the process is essential.

NOTES

Okay, let's talk about what people really want to know: how to make money doing whatever you want to do. Obviously, I am not a financial expert, so I cannot give financial advice. It would be amazing if I could tell you how to be a millionaire, but that is not a step I have achieved yet. However, we all have basic needs that have to be met. I have two decades of experience with affording a basic lifestyle without doing anything that I do not want to do. Daily grind drudgery just is not in my lexicon. Not that I have never had jobs that I hated, or quit in a panicked state of mind. Working in record stores, waiting tables in 24-hour diners, and hand shaking Mexican martinis to order were all jobs I had in high school and college. These were all jobs that gave me experience with my overall career decisions, making money, and paying bills. There are millions of people more successful than I am that you could get advice from that is perfect for you, but since you are here, I will tell you some of my tricks!

Twenty years ago I decided that, if I had to have a job, then I wanted to move to Los Angeles, roller skate around and design album covers like the guy in Xanadu. Once I had a Bachelor's degree in my hand (which, not one person has ever asked me if I had or was a prerequisite at any time during my entire career), I loaded up a small trailer full of stuff to make the move to LA. With $200 bucks saved in my pocket, one month's rent paid in advance for a room in a house with roommates I found online, and a pipe dream, I started my job hunt.

Jumping in a car and moving to a new city probably does sound a little risky for most people. Not that I would recommend this exact process to anyone. You certainly do not have to move to a bigger city than you live in right now to find success, but just as an example, this is how it worked out for me. I was lucky to quickly grab a coffee shop barista job in hopes that it would pay next month's rent while I searched for something more aligned with my creative career goals. What I did next is what I consider the "secret sauce" to obtaining a dream job.

Internships were my secret. I knew that I wanted to work in music, so I found three unpaid internships that I felt could get some experience, and get an inside view of different companies with nominal commitment. There was a poster print shop, a punk history magazine, and a record label that I landed. With these being unpaid internships, I knew that any one of these companies would not be put out if I decided to go with a paying position at another company. Also, I had found these internships without any reference or nepotism. These were internships advertised just looking for people interested in working for free. There are laws in every state that you should familiarize yourself with when deciding to accept an unpaid internship. They cannot make use of an unpaid intern to replace a real employee, and you must be learning something while you are on their premises. When looking for internships, you will be interviewing them for what you can learn from them, and to make sure they are not shady characters looking for free work. I assume they pick the person they feel has the most teachability promise. Obtaining an internship does not mean that you will automatically get a job. It's about getting a firsthand peek into an industry, possibly getting a reference for a future job application, and if you are lucky, being the first to apply for an entry level position if you love the company and want to work for them.

For me, it was instant love interning at a record label, and I put all my efforts into learning whatever possible there. I was so broke that I had to return a dollar can of chili to a grocery store to buy ten packs of ramen to eat for a few more days. Splurging only if I had to eat lunch out on a fountain drink and a dollar chicken sandwich from the gas station while filling up on gas only enough to get to that record label, and fingers-crossed hopefully home. I cannot fully tell you why it was so important for me to be there. At any moment, I could have gone to find a temp agency to place me at random places for a paycheck. I could have filled up my time with a restaurant job that paid well, or found a minimum wage record store job. Focusing on a dream job for me meant being on the inside, watching the magic happen, and just trying to find out how I could find a position for myself there.

As luck would have it, I did get a part-time position at that record label in the art department for $10 an hour. Then two weeks later, that part-time position became a $10 an hour full-time position. Then, a raise. Then, a salaried position. Ultimately working my way up to become Art Director of the department, and living on my own in my dream Silver Lake bungalow right in the middle of everything I found cool about Los Angeles. Passion and exhilaration does not even begin to explain the excitement that being at my desk working gave me. I would get to my desk two hours early, and stay working three hours late. I worked and worked and asked for more projects and responsibilities until it was time to leave that company onto the next stage of my career.

That was the paycheck revenue stage of my life. Next, I was going to learn about being a freelancer. "Being my own boss" was never that important to me. It was awesome having a job, and working with a team. There was just a nudge inside me that I needed to learn something more about money than just getting a paycheck every month. There was not much of a plan. I quit the record label, and every month I knew I needed to make enough money to pay my bills. Figuring out the client work game was my new assignment. There was a list of professional level skills under my belt, and I was ready to be hired. To make a long story short, I figured it out. Every month there seemed to be work, someone wanting to hire me, and I was able to pay my bills. I was still alive. I was not living under a bridge. Although it was fun being able to be a digital nomad working from anywhere in the world in my pajamas, it was not always easy. I had moments of wanting to take breaks from constantly needing new gigs. There were times when the idea of getting a corporate job again sounded so relaxing, but that never happened for me. I knew how to live with a salary, and survive as a freelancer without a consistent paycheck. That was great, but I knew I needed to learn something more.

The next phase of my financial development to learn how to make money starts getting a bit complicated. Things are finally starting to get interesting, but there is not a straight line from starting point to success. Projects that I have been slowly working on for years are just now starting to show glimmers of success. I cannot say I'm fully financially free just yet. However, I do have some big wins, and see epic possibilities unfolding in my path. It would be an absolute dream to one day share with everyone how to become a multimillionaire being who you are, but that will have to be another book.

For this book, I can only share my opinion of how to successfully create a game plan to monetize yourself. My implementation for creating an independent business life is taking financial education seriously, keeping my basic expenses extremely low, understanding revenue streams, and figuring out what revenue streams are going to be best for me to focus on while still doing what I want to do. Again, this is not financial advice. These are just basic ideas that you should think about while you are creating your own personal monetization plan.

There is a term that I hear financial gurus throw around when it comes to building wealth, and that term is "investor DNA." It is a good analogy for all the unique possibilities each human on Earth can choose to make money. Every single person can build a one-of-a-kind gameplan when it comes to how they feel comfortable making money. Some people have inherited knowledge and funds, some start with less than zero, some are risk takers and some people just play it safe. There are multiple revenue stream options and investment possibilities to choose from. How you build your revenue streams are custom to your needs, desires, skills, and security level that you want to build for yourself. Hopefully, taking a moment to think about all the revenue streams possible in the world helps you get some ideas of how you can become who you are with revenue streams and financial education!

Here are some revenue stream options to think about:

PAYCHECK REVENUE - We all know what it means to get a job, and get a paycheck for it. It worked for me at one time in life, and it could be for you!

SERVICE REVENUE - Service income is a range of tasks that you could do for someone else. It can cover a one-time need for a client like building a house. A service could be needed quarterly, like a haircut or accounting service. There are bi-annual jobs like teeth cleaning. There are monthly services, like a special software sold a service, or lawn care. It could be a daily service like a chef, dog-walker or courier. You could be an entertainer selling tickets to shows, or an educator selling seats to a class. The options are only limited by your imagination. Anything is possible. Having clients hire me for graphic design gigs and art direction worked for me for a decade of my career. It is a great way to work on your skills and try your own particular business ideas. Service revenue as a revenue stream that can bring you success at all levels. You could work from a laptop or a brick and mortar location. While you might be trading your time for money selling a service to a customer, there are a variety of levels of time commitments, intensity, and organization complexity to choose from.

PRODUCT REVENUE - Earning money from product sales can be super creative with unlimited options to create and choose from. Baked goods, paintings, furniture, toys, shirts, sandwiches, tools, spoons, shoes, vinyl records ect. You can make products yourself, have a manufacturer, or sell other companies' products. There are truly limitless options to sell items directly to a customer or make your products available for wholesale at a variety of price ranges and quantities.

DIGITAL PRODUCT REVENUE - Creating a digital product means you create a digital version of a physical product or an entirely new product digitally available directly to a customer. Digital products have the ability to be sold over and over again without having to recreate the work it took to generate the product. Some examples of digital products are online courses, software, stock photographs, audio books, video games, movies, etc.

ROYALTIES REVENUE - If you're a songwriter, author, or movie maker, you could be collecting royalties on a product you have created by allowing a more established company to sell the product directly to customers. Record labels, book publishers, and movie studios all have different ways they make deals with creators to help create, distribute and sell products. You could also franchise a brand or product that you own to another business for a win-win business deal. If you want to focus on royalties, it is not a bad idea, but you must research.

RENTAL REVENUE - Collecting rent is an awesome revenue stream that anyone can do with proper education and an idea. Every person is going to have their own rental real estate style and methods. There are a million different ways to get started, and a million ways to be successful at it. If rental income feels like something you may want to do, start the research!

AFFILIATE INCOME AND SALES REVENUE - There are people that sell other people's products for a cut of a portion of the sales profits. I am sure you have seen many influencers do this online. From watching all sorts of advice videos on this topic, it seems this is an effortless monetizing process for some, and an impossible dream for others. I think the important thing to remember is that people make money from this process in a fun and authentic way. If this is something that you want to have as a revenue stream in your life, it is a possible dream.

AD REVENUE AND SPONSORSHIPS - There are mega influencers and micro influencers making money with direct brand deals, and from advertisers paying to place advertisements on content that gets online traffic. There are writers, video creators, social media influencers, and podcast hosts creating custom commercials for brands as a revenue stream. If this revenue stream resonates with your goals add it to your monetization plan.

DIVIDENDS REVENUE - Some people like to invest in companies to obtain cash or stock dividend income. If this is something that excites you, explore the process and possibilities.

CAPITAL GAINS REVENUE - The tax collector in your country would be a good place to start researching what is considered a capital gain or loss. The most common capital gain that people know about is when you make money from the sale of a house or commercial property. In my opinion, that is an awesome revenue stream. Capital gains or losses also happen when you sell cryptocurrency, stocks, bonds, precious metals, and property. Understanding tax law is important to this revenue stream, so start researching and learning as soon as possible.

NEW IDEAS FOR REVENUE STREAMS - There is always room for new ideas in this world. Anything is possible. Start creating your own custom revenue stream plan to become who you are.

I could go on for days talking about monetization ideas for making an income based on individual business styles and dream routines, but let's wrap this up. Creating your own income plan is not easy, and does take time. Sometimes, decades. Take some time to organize your own monetization plan. Perhaps have two or three income roadmaps. Layout methods for a minimum earnings plan up to your highest wealth aspirations blueprint. Revisit that plan with every step that you fail, succeed, and learn to experience growth. Motivate and embolden yourself while you research, build, and plan ahead to achieve greatness. Success is relative to everyone's individual opinion. If you would like my definition of success, it is simply to have the luxury of doing whatever you want to do everyday. I believe that can happen at low and high income levels. It is not easy, but something a person can create with a customized monetization financial plan and effective spending habits.

Everyone has a personal brand. Even if you did not want one, you have got a personal brand. And, yes, it is possible to have a personal brand without being on the internet. What is your reputation in the workplace, in your neighborhood, at friend's parties? If people are going to be thinking about you, talking about you, sharing who you are with others, and what it is that you do, you have a personal brand. Let's take the time to consider fine-tuning what your personal brand is. While you are at it, let's go ahead and try to make it easy and clear for others to decipher your personal brand and communicate it with others.

For some this is a nightmare to think about, and for others, it is a dream assignment. When you are a multi-hyphenate, multi-passionate, multi-skilled professional person with a variety of interests, it certainly is a hard task. Not to mention, your personal brand is going to shift and modify with time as you fail, succeed, and become who you are.

If I am meeting someone new and they ask the dreaded "what do you do?" question, I immediately look for an escape route. I take a deep breath, and try my best to evaluate the kind of answer each individual might be searching for. I know I am about to sound like a crazy lady trying to rattle off a million things that I do which may or may not generate profit. Usually when people ask that question, I translate that to mean they want to know, "How do you make money?" Depending on the time of the year, sometimes I don't even know how I make money. There are situations when I feel as if I will never make any sense to a normal human being, and there are times when I feel like peas in a pod with a group of professional creatives. Ultimately, I do want to communicate and connect with people, and I believe having an organized personal brand is a part of that process. This book that you are reading right now is a technique in improving myself to develop and craft my own personal brand presentation and communication. Writing, as a brand connection expression style may not be for everyone. However, writing is certainly something anyone can experiment with in a range of categories, products, and skill levels.

Just to be clear, a personal brand does not mean that one must be selling something. Think about all the mega superstars and micro famous people in the world that you are aware of and have enjoyed their brand without handing over any money to purchase something. Most of us have never purchased a product from people with personal branding success. They created their own way to make a profit being themselves. Brand yourself, and figure out your own way. Do not be afraid to give your talents away for free. Do not be afraid to charge a fee for value that you bring to others. If you are doing an honest job that brings value to anyone in any way, there is a unique solution for you to brand yourself; and make a living doing it.

Also remember, you do not have to do this perfectly. You do not need to be a professional online influencer. You do not need to be a marketing genius. Simply just start with organizing in your mind what you love, what your skills are, and how you personally are going to make the world a better place. The presentation of it all will come naturally as you present yourself in-person and online. Plus, always remember to not be afraid to change and rebrand yourself as you grow! A personal brand is not just a label to categorize you into a box forever, but an original metamorphosis of becoming who you are.

While you are establishing your personal brand, there are a few things that you might want to get out of your head and onto a piece of paper. How do you want to communicate with others? These are traits that you might want to constantly change up forever as you change, and some traits that you know in your heart will always be totally you using a brand voice. Think about what is the tone of your brand voice that you want people to perceive when you communicate with them? Are you a loving mother type? Are you a wild best friend type? Are you a funny grumpy old grandpa type? Are you a sharp-lounge know-it-all young kid type? Are you a dark, mysterious, trench-coat wearing, smoking-in-the-rain stranger type? Are you the no nonsense personal coach type? You create your own voice. You simply try to embody that voice in your communication materials as much as possible. It's not about being fake. This is not about picking a single "niche" or personality trait that never changes, but rather picking a communication style that is authentic and memorable. Maybe your voice is someone who has a new emotion every minute. This is a way to organize your personal brand communication in your head. A brand voice is not just about speaking, but also the tone you use in written communications as well.

The next thing you might want to think about is if you want a personal brand logo, colors, and fonts associated with your personal brand. Do you have to do this? Nope. Do you want to do this? Probably. Why the heck not? It is so fun to take it to the next level. However, being a graphic designer, I can make all this junk for myself as often as I want for free. If I had to pay for graphic design, I may just skip this part too! I will try not to ramble too long about this part, but I have got to let you know my tips and tricks on this just in case it is helpful. Also, keep in mind, trends change when it comes to branding and graphic design. With each generation and decade comes new technology, styles, and opinions. A twenty year-old graphic designer will have different styles of communication design as an eighty year-old graphic designer. Ultimately, a graphic designer's job is to make the client happy. Do what you love, and feel cool. Those are the only rules I think are important when it comes to a personal brand.

A logo is not a brand. I'm not really sure why people are so logo-obsessed. You do not need a logo to be successful, and a logo can be updated or re-branded at any time. Creating a logo should not be a stressful task. If you are going to have a logo then there are some classic logo design rules to consider while you are designing. The classic way of designing a logo is that your logo should be readable quarter-size. I was told in logo design class to imagine if a business card was on the floor, and you were standing up looking down at it. A person should be able to recognize a logo printed that small from that distance. With social media changing how we consume brand identity and design, logos now need to be readable and recognizable much smaller, and at a lower digital dots per inch resolution. A computer screen is much less sharp than real life, and phone screens are even smaller. Logos now need to be designed with that in mind. Imagine the tiniest little spot on a web browser bar, the favicon spot. Now that is tiny! If a logo can go that small and still be recognizable, that is freaking awesome for you! Your logo communication is on point! It is not totally necessary to be that small, but you get the idea. Being unmistakably instantly recognized at any size is the goal.

In my opinion, there is no need to get crazy working on a logo for months or pay thousands of dollars on a logo design just to get started. It's not a crime to start simple with the simple idea you have right now, because you can revamp or level up your logo at any moment. A logo can be a graphic symbol solution or a font solution. As a rule, a logo needs to be recognizable in a black or white version of the logo, as well as in your approved brand colors. If someone requests your logo artwork for any reason, you need to have a color version file, a black version for light backgrounds file, and a white version file for dark backgrounds. Have all three color version files of your logo easily accessible to use or send out when needed in the file type requested.

Another thing to consider that might be even more important than having a personal brand logo, is to have a nice high resolution press photo of yourself prepared and ready for that exciting moment when someone might ask for an approved press photo of yourself.

It can be a good idea to pick a set of colors, textures or creative style you want people to correlate with when they think of you. You could go simple and pick one or two colors to associate with your personal brand for a website and business cards. You could also use textures to correlate your brand with things like corduroy, sequins, or feathers. Do you want to always wear bright neon outfits? Do you want to wear black leather studded punk belts and rock rainbow hair until you are ninety two years old? Do you want to wear glasses, smoking a pipe next to a fireplace while sitting in a vintage brown leather chair? Do you exclusively wear black with bright red lipstick? All of these things could be color, texture or style choices for a personal brand. Come up with your own unique ideas to communicate your personal brand style.

When it comes to fonts, there are probably a trillion fonts you could choose from, or you can design your own fonts. Constantly using the same fonts to communicate a brand's message can feel a little boring. Over a long period of time using the same fonts consistently will give a soothing look and feel to your brand. My suggestion is that you pick two fonts that are available on your computer or phone you own right now, and stick with those fonts exclusively until you are able to afford professional design help for every single piece of content you create. Don't try to get fancy if it's going to hold you back or keep you from using the same fonts consistently on content. Most professional designers will choose a serif font, like "Times" and a san-serif font, like "Arial" for design collateral. Both font types seem to compliment each other when using them together. A third font choice to add to your brand font choice collection would be to a handwritten, cursive script, or decorative style of font. There are no real rules you have to follow. Make whatever you want. It's all just communication design suggestions. There is no graphic design police that will write you a ticket for bad design. If you like something, you like it. Go with whatever you choose. Personally, I like using classic traditional fonts for long term use in brand design pieces. They have worked for the greats for decades, and those design materials using classic fonts seem to stay cool and relevant longer than pieces that I have seen using trendy fonts.

Now think about where you want your personal brand to show up, hangout, and be found? Where are the people hanging out that you want to meet? Do you need to show and participate in local physical venues, on certain social media platforms, or possibly just broadcast a show from your living room. Find those places you want to be, and make it easy for people to discover you, connect with you, and share your personal brand with others.

There are probably going to be tons of moments when you might compare your personal brand to others that are more fancy and more successful. Truly, just take that feeling and throw it out of the window. Be inspired by others when you feel that tug of jealousy or that urge to feel less superior. Put a note on your goal list to revamp, reorganize and take you from the level it is now to the next level. I do not believe in competition when it comes to personal brands. No one can be "you" better than you, and we are all at different levels of our success journey. Your unique style of communication, mentoring, inspiration, products or value is something so special. Nothing compares to you! What's your thing? What makes you different? Who inspires you? Do you have any heroes that you can model your personal brand from? You don't need to copy, but having personal brand role models that make you feel cool can help when deciding how you will present yourself. Developing a personal brand might not come naturally to everyone, but we all start somewhere. Get to thinking, planning and organizing how you want to present yourself to the world.

Take some time to answer some of these personal branding organization questions for yourself:

What is your current mission in life?

What are your talents and professional skills?

What are your core values?

What are some possibilities of how you might achieve your mission?

What are five emotions you want people to feel when they think of you?

What are three adjectives you would like people to use when describing you?

What type of friends or customers would you like to attract?

What type of problems does your personal brand solve?

What is your personality tone of your personal brand voice?

What makes you different?

What are your favorite colors?

What font styles do you like?

Do you want a personal brand logo?

If someone were to interview you right now, what three topics would make a good story about you?

Do you make it easy for new people to discover your personal brand and contact you?

Where will you position your personal brand?

Can you make a list of people or companies you would love to collaborate with to achieve more goals?

Can you make a list of 10 personal brands that currently seriously inspire you?

Is Social Media important? In 2007, I probably would have said, "OMG, social media is everything. Go have fun!" In 2018, I probably would have said, "you have to be on social media if you are serious about marketing and being a brand. Go create content as professional as possible." In 2020, I probably would have said, "just put a camera in your face immediately, and start talking! No one cares what you look like, just show up and start." However, today, my response to social media being important is… "meh."

Don't get me wrong. I love people using social media in a creative way just for fun as well as for business. I absolutely adore all the people in the world adding content to the internet that connects them with like-minded people. It is amazing! The internet is making it possible and much easier for so many people in the world to become who they are.

It's like an ever-growing real-time library of humans that we all can contribute to instantly, so that we can learn and share with each other. I love how people can instantly be investigative reporters, documentary filmmakers, writers, recording artists, and teachers. There are an endless number of occupations that anyone can decide they want to try out and make money doing, whatever their mind can come up with. Did I say it was amazing? It is amazing!

I used to see social media as a necessity to present yourself or your brand on the internet. Although being on social media still has its benefits and value, I do feel a shift in how important it is. Do you feel it, too? I mean we are less than 20 years into social media existing in a major way in human history, so I am sure there will be ups and downs with how we all engage with it. What the average person is gaining from social media is becoming more defined right now, as we speak. It started out being fun and exciting, then got more professional, and now we are seeing a trend of social media being more casual. Sometimes, I feel like social media platforms are just going to be a bunch of people selling stuff to other people selling stuff. It is hard to imagine what the average person gets out of it when algorithms do not show actual content to followers or subscribers, yet they are being bombarded with obvious, unwanted, annoying advertisements. I see that people are really evaluating what they are actually getting out of it versus the time spent on it to determine how much they will be using it.

Most social media users are getting more savvy with how and why they are using it. Some people are ditching it altogether. Some people are being more private with their content. Some people are only using it if it brings in a profit of some kind. Some people are ditching the mega social media corporations for micro social media platforms to get information that is hyperfocused on very specific interests. I do see the value in social media, but I also see the value in not actually using it at all. I have come to a new perspective for the current significance of social media platforms. Social media gives us entertainment, education, inspiration, and friendships. I do not see it as a necessity anymore.

Obviously, having a little or a lot of likes, followers, or views isn't everything. There are a ton of prosperous careers with zero need to advertise, get customers or clients, or have a reason to be online to be a success. Sure, social media makes it easy to share by word of mouth the cool stuff we are doing and the cool stuff we personally like. So, while it's super helpful to make content that is easily shareable, if you don't want to be on social media, you simply do not have to. It seems like a hard task, but think of all the successful businesses and personal brands that exist without being on major social platforms. Heck, some do not even have websites. Your local gas station or dry cleaners could be profiting a million dollars a year for decades, and never even considered opening a social media profile. As time goes by, social media is valuable, but does not seem to be everything.

I have been around and using social media since it was created; probably naively. I feel very lucky to remember life without the internet, and fortunate to see how human interaction changed as the internet unfolded. When social media happened it was very exciting, and there are probably a million interesting changes in human development that happened which I do not even realize at this very moment. For example, I saw the death of the "band flyer." Before social media, you would design a poster for your band's show, and then go find a copy machine. You would make copies of the poster for the wall of the venue and local hangouts like coffee shops. Then, you would make a bunch of four-per-page copies, and hand-cut the smaller versions to personally hand out to people you would run across out in the world. That seemed to change overnight. It was magic to simply make a post on a platform where one thousand of your friends would instantly see that you had a show coming up. That simple task cut out hours of work. At the time it felt amazing. People actually engaged with the online "band flyer" post, and more people knew about your band, and it did seem like more people would come to the show. It was effortless, simple, and felt organic; until it wasn't. There came a point when a social media page for a local band didn't get much engagement, even with a good size chunk of their very own social media "followers" they collected. There started to brew an ominous feeling building for local bands using social media to promote shows. Your page would only get eyeballs on your posts if you paid money to a mega corporation to share the posts. The time spent building those organic relationships and building a band social media page started to feel like wasted time. Social media was "free," right? What local bands had an advertising budget? A local band was lucky to cover their practice space rent for the month with door money from a show. Not all bands, but most bands I've come across do not make enough money to earn a living wage for all band members, much less have an advertising budget.

This feeling of having a social platform "ghost" or "shadow ban" your posts from your own followers was deflating. Bands, small brands and small businesses having similar problems didn't stop using social media, but I believe everyone got a little more creative with their content techniques to keep it free. People realized social media platforms could pull the rug right from under you, so you needed to be strategic with how much each company controlled your audience connection. Ultimately, I think this happened for everyone at different times, in different cities, and by different age groups of users. Sequentially, I think from the excitement phase to the realization phase (that social media platforms own your audience), it was clear we all needed to organize how important social media marketing actually is bringing to our lives and businesses. How much time and effort was worth it to use social media?

It is sad that we have lost something worthwhile by not meeting in-person as much as we did in the 90s, pre-internet. That's not to say that I think social media has no value or is destroying humanity. There is something so monumental about how unique and personalized social media is helping people create independent incomes and lifestyles. Someone who has no memory of life before social media is probably going to have a different approach and instincts when it comes to the future of social media's popularity and purpose. All ages should be genuinely considered and included in the conversation as time goes on. We all experience technology together, but from different generational experiences and lenses. Truthfully, at this exact moment, most elements of social media feel a little boring to me. However, there is a glimmer of excitement that I feel for what is about to happen next. Whatever may unfold.

I used to spend hours creating elaborate digital marketing plans for myself and clients with the best of intentions to do it all. I thought it was important to be on every single popular platform. As each new social platform rolled out… add it to the to-do list! I seriously thought a person needed to spend every waking hour, and do everything as humanly possible to market their own business on social media. If you didn't, you must just not want it bad enough. I think this mentality was appropriately named "hustle culture." That might work for some, but I am so glad I do not live in that mindset anymore. That is not to say that working hard and long hours does not pay off. Sometimes all nighters, and working an extra five hours a day to hone skills is the only way to get better. It is more about taking the approach to not chase what everyone else is doing and to spend more time evaluating what is appropriate and most time efficient for the prize you are hoping to win.

I've taken a step back, and have gained a new philosophy when dealing with the current climate of social media. I calmly apply these main intentions to my personal efforts and approach to social media. Does using social media add valuable skill building to my life? Am I learning by engaging online, and not just being a wallflower wishing I could get into the game? Am I fulfilling life dreams and having fun using social media? Can I build a social media management schedule for myself that consistently feels authentic, fun, and relaxing? Am I making content that I am going to love forever, or content that is going to dissolve into oblivion the next day. These are my questions I ask myself coming from the perspective that there is probably no advertising budget or team of employees to farm out tasks to. I recommend coming up with your own list of thoughtful personal investigation and non-negotiables for creating your own creative internet social dreams.

Just as a random side-note, I like to research successful vintage marketing that worked throughout time. I like to know about all the advantageous marketing that happened in the 1800s, in the 1920's, the 50's, and the 80's. There are great books and videos about marketing throughout the decades. Classic marketing can bring interesting perspectives to this day. I think about all the successful people who are still successful today that never had the opportunity to use social media. Shakespeare doesn't have a social media account, but people make content to share their love for Shakespeare in their own way everyday. Not to mention, humans have shared Shakespeare's work decade after decade worldwide without the internet ever existing. Now this may even be a further tangential side-note, but I often think about how Shakespeare's works are all in the public domain. It is kind of mindblowing how much money people all over the world are earning from creating unique products from his original works. If Shakespeare were alive today, he could still personally be making a huge income from his work done centuries ago, simultaneously giving free access to anyone who wishes to also make income from his works. Okay, we've traveled too far from the point. Just something to think about.

If social media isn't your thing, then that is totally cool. Don't mess around with it. Just work on whatever you want to work on without it and keep building! If social media is making you feel bad about yourself, remember you don't have to be on it to be successful. You can just use it for fun and creativity without expectations. If you are using social media for the clicks, views, and likes, I do not want to ridicule that process as if I know what works for every personality. High competitive stress to "win" could be valuable for some. There are people out there that love the grind. Ultimately, I feel as long as you are working towards a better "you" becoming who you are, you can define and design your own unique lifestyle methods using social media to grow.

Before I was of legal drinking age, I witnessed a friend's band have some mainstream success in the 90's. They had a music video playing on television, a song on major alternative rock radio (not just a local college radio station), and all for a debut EP release. They were under twenty one, and watching them "make it" gave me the impression that achieving your dreams in the world must be so easy if you just go for it. No problem. Life must be easy like Sunday morning, I just had to go out there and carpe diem. Well… I don't want to burst any wide-eyed adorable heart bubbles. As I grew up I realized, it's not that easy for most. Not to mention, sometimes it can be painful to have your greatest "proof" of success happen in your youth while you spend decades in the building phase of your next successful moment. I certainly know that feeling all too well. I have lovingly dubbed it "failure fatigue" for myself to acknowledge the feeling, and then make myself keep working without any recognition of achievement. In spite of that, it does actually feel good to know it is not impossible for big dreams to materialize into reality.

Something that always stuck with me from that time was watching the singer of that band be interviewed. I would reference that interview here, but I cannot seem to find it anywhere. So, I guess it is lost in internet rabbit holes or just exists in my memory. Anyway, the singer was asked what all the band's success felt like. When describing what it was like to be experiencing these big moments, opening for huge bands with massive crowds so early in a career, she stated that she felt like she was an Antenna. She talked about having their songs played on radio stations all over the world, standing on stages with all the people connecting with her energy, and then connecting with all of their energy made her feel like she was an antenna. Be an antenna. I thought that is what I wanted to feel. That is what I wanted to be, an antenna.

While thinking about how to use energy to manifest a destiny, it makes sense that you need to harness all the energy exuding from your brain as you externalize your personality and your creations. Plus, consider all the outside energy directed at you that you want to embrace, and all that energy you want to dodge while you are having your life experiences. And, although it would be nice to be a real rockstar, even for just five minutes, I don't think you need to be a rockstar or necessarily even famous to be an antenna. Simply broadcasting your best talent, heart, mind, and soul out there to the world in a way that feels energizing seems like a good enough idea and such a powerful energy exchange. I would not even get all caught up with worrying about broadcasting to the entire world. If singing a lullaby to a baby brings an immeasurable amount of importance and high-quality of life to a person that cannot understand or comprehend yet, just think of what is possible if you release your talents out into the world. No matter how "cringe" you think you are, I bet there is one person who actually loves it and is inspired.

I imagine broadcasting could be simply a person that has unique knowledge teaching someone else how to do something they want to learn. For example, a chef sharing how they make a modernized classic recipe, a guitar player teaching their unique guitar solo techniques, or an open-mic comedian trying out some jokes for the first time. Broadcasting to one person is just as important as broadcasting to the entire world. Having a clear strategy of goals, dream routines, and a list of broadcasting activities which feel authentic is a great launch pad to start achieving some aspirations. Add to that, checking-in constantly with yourself to see if your goals have changed, being open to how life unfolds, building new skills and trying new exciting things, then you are consciously being the architect of your lifestyle.

There are many ways to broadcast yourself. We have talked about using social media, and the million ways to do that, or choosing not to if it does not feel valuable. You could broadcast yourself by making your own product or services for people to experience. That could be books, music, creating events, teaching one-on-one, or anything creative you could think of. The ideas are limitless. Broadcasting could be opening a beloved local pizza shop, crafting beer, or building a go-kart arcade. Broadcasting yourself does not just have to mean hosting a radio show or being in front of a camera all the time. It just has to mean sharing who you are with the world. Share your thoughts and energy, to then receive the thoughts and energy from others that make life uniquely curated and memorable.

A third way you could broadcast yourself is by using press media. I would not say that using press to share what you are doing with the world is leveling-up. Press does not automatically give you more authority, expertise or influence. Press is simply a way to broadcast a message. Some people are really good at landing press opportunities even if they are not the best in their field, and you have to remember that some people pay millions of dollars to get press that gets little to no attention. Personally, I would stay away from the thought that press is about showing off, and move towards the idea that press is a relationship. You are building a relationship with the person or press outlet giving you the opportunity to share your "thing" respectfully to their audience. Then, if you are lucky, you have entered into the lexicon of someone in that audience's mind in a way they want to learn more about you.

When getting fancy press for yourself, you might gain a new fan, or you may get a bunch of people who forget about you five minutes later. On the other hand, someone could come across your interview from a podcast that has two listeners. One of those listeners could decide to follow your career journey forever. I have witnessed a high-dollar first-rate seasoned publicist do her magic making a product go from zero recognition to being featured in major publications. Investing in a skillful and accomplished publicist can translate to millions in sales when you are ready. Paying for press can work, but we can all realistically DIY (do-it-yourself) our own press plans until a press media budget is an option.

I am not a publicist, so take what you will from my opinions on getting press with a grain of salt. When you are acting as your own publicist in this current climate, treat your press relationships like you would treat people at the office that you really like. Be helpful to them, by bringing something to the table that is interesting to discuss. Go out and look for press outlets that might be interested in knowing you for longer than just a day, and make their job easier by bringing them fully complete interesting stories to run with. Maybe even think of the press media as a brand collaborations. Think about how your brand can benefit their brand, and if there is a win-win moment you can share. Next, all you can do is pitch your press release or idea to them and see what comes of it.

The internet has made it possible to share anything with the potential to reach anybody in the world at any moment. My view is that a first-time journalist is just as valuable to the world as a seasoned professional, so if someone reaches out to you for an interview say yes. Say yes to everyone until you physically cannot say yes to all the publicity requests coming into your inbox. Which would obviously be a fantastic problem to have. In the most likely seriaro it is going to be you pitching yourself to press media for some time. It is totally okay to submit yourself to publications, shows and other content outlets that you feel your story is a value match for their audience. The worst that could happen is that you get ignored.

There are many different degrees of press outlet statuses and types. There is the guy in mom's basement internet show. There is the friend's blog. There is the local free magazine found at supermarkets. There is the cult indie zine based on the perfect genre. There is that fun morning show on the local news. There are the college indie radio stations. From online press, to print press, to television press, and beyond, there is a starting level that you can begin pitching yourself to. As you get more experience with your DIY press plan you can pitch to bigger and bigger press opportunities regionally, nationally, and internationally. There may come a point when you feel as if you are ready to hire a professional publicist. When that time arrives, you should find someone with a ton of recommendations and proof of work that you can probe and verify they can deliver the results you are possibly investing in for a three month publicity campaign.

Now for some actionable tips from my approach to DIY press. Take these questions and answer them as they might apply. Everyone's plan of attack and demands are going to be different. Keep an on-going list of small and big press outlets you resonate with. Try to book yourself with a mountain of interviews on your calendar, or just book one at a time as is realistically manageable for you to commit to. And remember, if someone does choose to interview you, stay connected in a reasonable amount of time with a new press release or reason to come back to share something new with that person.

What things are you working on in your life that could be story worthy?

What is interesting about you beyond having a new product, service or event?

What are some creative ways you can build a buzz for what's on your plate beyond traditional press?

What is your presentation process going to look like?

Do you have a media kit?

Do you have a press release plan and procedure?

Are you easily found online, and clearly articulated who you are?

Do you have professional examples of how someone you admire manages their press?

Here is a little press idea list brainstorm to start pitching yourself today. Make a list of a variety of press outlet types, and the person's contact name you would love to pitch a story idea to. Try a realistic list and a dream list. Then, write down your story pitch. Believe in yourself!

TV SHOWS -

NEWSPAPERS -

MAGAZINES -

PODCASTS -

ONLINE VIDEO SHOWS -

COLLABORATION IDEAS -

BLOGS -

EVENTS -

VALUABLE STORY PITCH ONE:

WRITE A SHORT PARAGRAPH BIOGRAPHY WITH THE MOST RELEVANT INFORMATION FOR THE PITCH:

VALUABLE STORY PITCH TWO:

WRITE A SHORT PARAGRAPH BIOGRAPHY WITH THE MOST RELEVANT INFORMATION FOR THE PITCH:

VALUABLE STORY PITCH THREE:

WRITE A SHORT PARAGRAPH BIOGRAPHY WITH THE MOST RELEVANT INFORMATION FOR THE PITCH:

When you have a personal brand, you may not have "customers" per se. Not everyone with a personal brand has something to sell. You could have an audience of some kind with fans that you may or may not know personally. You may just be well known in your town for what you do. Maybe, it is just friends and family who get to experience and appreciate you for what you bring to the table. I think it is beneficial to be mindful of what the perks are for hanging out with you. This could also be your personal brand mission statement.

A mission statement for a business is usually a short statement about what they do, why they exist, and how they bring value. You spend your entire life being you, why not have your own mission statement? Personally, I do not always know what I am doing and why, but I know I have one main goal when someone hangs out with me. My daydream mission statement is that I want anyone hanging out with me to believe in themselves a little more; and be inspired to do what they want to do everyday. Does that happen one hundred percent of the time with every person I meet? Probably not. Do I annoy some people by always looking on the brightside? Probably. Does everyone love me all the time, and never get mad at me? No. But, I know that

I have a mission. If people do not want to connect and associate with me, that's cool. I will continue to do my thing, hoping to bring value to the people currently in my galaxy. Now I ask you, what is your mission statement, and what are some perks for your customers, fans and friends?

Like uniqueness, perks help you stand out from the crowd and bring a benefit to others. When you are becoming who you are, and creating a brand that is totally unique to you, then you want to give people a perk as a thank you for the energy exchange for love, attention, and/or money. I use the work "perk," because it feels light and easy. A perk could be something simple as a daily giggle, making someone's life more manageable, or inspiration to take on the world.

It is meaningful for someone to walk anyway with something after they get-together with you. There are a million creative ideas to come up with giving unique perks for various reasons. You could give perks for taking the time to discover you, repeatedly coming together, or investing in your brand. Here is a list of potential interactions that could be reasons to create perks for your brand.

First Discovery: The first discovery of your brand is when someone realizes you exist. Someone may come across your video thumbnail, walk by your shop, see your album cover looking through the vinyl stacks, or they may get an email from a friend recommending your services. Whatever the reason someone might discover you, what is the thing they walk away with as a "thank you" for checking you out? Is it inspiration? Is it entertainment? Did they learn something? Is it a tiny free gift? Was it a bite-size sample? Hoping people resonate and remember you is always a goal, but I would say the first discovery is more of a "thank you for checking me out" moment. Think about how you can incorporate that into your personal brand.

What is something free or affordable to give someone for discovering you? In high school, I worked at a record store that had a music bar. No drinks were served, but only a set of ten stools and ten headphones stations. My job was to "professionally" open CD jewel cases, place CDs in the corresponding stereo for the customer to listen to their pick for free as long as they wanted to sit there and listen. Then, I would shrink wrap that CD back up, and put it back on the storeroom floor as if nothing happened if they decided not to purchase it. This was probably not the best business plan in the world. However, it was a creative idea to market a record store experience directly to the snobbiest of music snobs that would probably be their ideal customer to buy a CD. It was truly a dream to be able to listen to every record you were ever curious for free at any moment. I started at A in the pop/rock section, and went all the way to Z listening to as many records as possible. That was a lot of time spent at a record store. Which is why it just made sense for me to work there, even though I could have made double or triple the wage working at another type of business. This was simply a moment I recognized giving something valuable for free does connect customers to your experience.

I think we all get the concept of complimentary samples. Who does not love a free sample. Brainstorm some ideas you could do. Can you offer a free book, worksheet, or webinar? Can you give an online gallery of your work that is fun to look through as entertainment or inspiration? Can you give tips or how-to videos based on your skills? There are many brands that connect with an audience with a commodity that is absolutely free forever for people to enjoy, and never have a reason to purchase something from that brand. For example, a podcast, music videos, or hilarious social media posts. Your main value proposition for your personal brand can be free for a first-time observer to a long-time follower. It is all about how you feel most comfortable setting up your revenue streams, and what is possible for you.

Get creative. The main takeaway here is to be grateful and thank all who come across you to leave with a little gift thoughtfully designed by you.

First Time Buyer: Getting a first time buyer is definitely not easy and a congratulatory moment. You have got someone to find your offer valuable enough to make a purchase. You have made that human exchange of something relevant and beneficial. It is awesome! How will you thank them? Do you have an added free bonus? Do you have a coupon available for their next purchase? Do you have a special meet up party for your customers to mingle and interact? How will you give and stay connected with someone that has taken that next step to get to know you a little better with making a purchase? Sometimes it is easy to get that sale, and move on to your next task. Maybe your first time buyers fade away quietly into the night, but try not to be the one "ghosting" customers. Figure out your own method to bring that extra perk for continuing to stay associated with you.

Staying Connected: When it is official, and you have someone that wants to be a regular consumer of your universe, how will you stay on their mind in a meaningful way? You could send them hundreds of emails they ignore from a mailing list they pretended to want to be on. A social media management company or digital marketing agency could provide you with a full regimen to adhere to for everything you are supposed to be doing considering the current tech trends. For whatever the most contemporary techniques are, I am sure there is a basic right way and a barely functional way to keep a follower relationship going. Sure, having a well-managed email list is great if you know how to do it, but not everyone has that skill set to manage it well. Hiring the most cutting edge perfect digital marketing team or social media manager to help you is great if you have the budget. Sorry if it sounds as if I am hating on all the super high-end, professional ways brands stay connected. I get frustrated with companies overcharging for little results, and know-it-alls. Professional level marketing is a valuable service. It is a real position within a company reserved for brands that have the ability to hire employees. The reality is, most of us are not there yet. When it comes to personal brands, it can be tempting to hire someone to solve problems and get over hurdles, but I have seen a lot of people hire professionals for little results that do not recoup expenses. Just be aware. It could take a solid decade of building up your brand on your own before you get to that magical moment of hiring professional help. Then, figuring out the right person or company to hire is also a cultivated craft. The bright side of staying connected on your own is that even professionals get it wrong sometimes. No one knows everything or has all the answers. If you are starting from scratch with one fan, or have a crowd of patrons that want to stay connected, it is possible to come up with something engaging that is doable and practical for you to manage. Your ideas, building skills, and the time you have to manage your community is going to be your guide to finding your sweet spot.

If you are going to be your own community manager and social event coordinator, let's think about personalizing your own get-together style. There are book clubs in person or online. There are listening parties. You could plan monthly Q&A live streams for people that want to talk directly to you. You could host parties with themes relevant to your brand at restaurants, bars, movie theaters, or parks. Think of brand experiences in terms of what you think is fun and worthwhile. Staying on someone's mind, and having them mark a date to attend your event is the main goal. If hangouts and events happen consistently daily, weekly, monthly, or annually, and becomes something of a habit to join in on your thing, then you've got a solid plan to be remembered and stay connected.

Repeat Customer: The warmest fuzziest moment happened! A stranger checked you out. Decided to enjoy your work or product. You stayed on their mind, and they have returned to consume again. I would say that is proof you have made a positive impact on someone's life. You might just have a fan if you play your cards right!

Now that the information is in and you have confirmation your idea could be a new revenue stream for you. This could be the moment when you make your next-level plans of where you want to move your brand forward. There are no rules that say you have to grow to maximum profitability as soon as possible. Easing into success just might have a better outcome versus being an overnight sensation. I have seen people with mega fire brands that seemingly come out of nowhere. They get to a monumental level of success only to make the decision to step it back a few notches. Consciously designing your day and making financial decisions to make sure you do not lose it all means maturely making the decision to go at your own pace. Some people will have instant success. Some people will have waves of success and failure. Your story is going to be your story. Your journey is going to take however long it takes.

Your repeat customer phase could be the time to get digital marketing or SEO professional help, or you may stay in the do-it-yourself era for a while. Either way, while you are implementing your marketing campaigns, it is still a good idea to focus on consistent community events, a high-quality experience, and perks that bring them back annually, monthly, weekly or daily. Perhaps make a list of all the companies you seem to frequent, and why you are attracted to them. What makes a coffee shop your favorite place to stop? Why is your local pizza shop the only place you will order pizza from? How does a cleaning service company gain trust? Why do you religiously listen to every episode of certain podcasts, and why do you just occasionally listen to others that you like? Decipher and analyze your own tastes, and the preferences of the people you attract might be comparable.

While you are engaging with your community, keep it easy, bring value, and make it worth their while to come back again with ease. Being available, reliable, and staying connected is a gift enough for most repeat customers. Stay close to your vision for your brand. Keep building on the quality of what you bring to the table, keep trustworthiness high. and you should be good to grow!

Super Fan: You may not know what a super fan is. A super fan is going to buy any product that you release. The super fan wants all the albums, all the Japanese imports, and covers their walls with all the posters. They want to binge every episode, and watch all the behind the scenes interviews. A super fan buys tickets to every concert they can afford to go to, and will buy more than just one concert tee shirt from the merch booth. Simply purchasing something from you is entertainment for a super fan. A super fan can easily be taken advantage of, and a super fan is something to protect and cherish beyond all things in your control. If you are truly blessed to have a super fan, you have got to do your best to make the most ethically correct decisions when going about your business.. It is true what they say "with great power comes great responsibility."

I've heard famous people say, they could sign 1000 autographs, and if they don't sign 1001 autographs, then they are a jerk. Yes, you have got to be realistic with your capabilities. How you connect and appreciate super fans is going to be unique to your resources. There are a million ideas of how you can make super fans feel special. Having this level of admiration might not be experienced by everyone, but it's just something to think about if it ever happens to you.

NOTES

No one is good at everything. Even big dreamers have to be realistic about what we can actually do all alone. Being self-aware is something that is going to be a huge help along the way of becoming who you are. Ask for help, take a class, build a team, lean on someone, or assign tasks to others. Everyone is going to have road blocks to overcome, and we must remember that humans are lifelong learners. Sometimes we need teachers or professionals to help us get over bigger problems that we cannot handle alone with the knowledge we currently possess. There is no shame in it. We just have to be self-aware, prepare, and make plans accordingly. There are a million different ways you can join forces with others or simply learn from others to grow in personal and business life.

When you are building something on your own, and you don't have an office full of people to interact with daily, sometimes you feel a little crazy. When you are becoming who you are, it can feel lonely. The good news is you are not stranded on a desert island. Sure, you can do everything on your own and be happy and thrive. People do it on their own all the time. However, some of us do need help to become more advanced. You are going to be the one to decipher what you need to advance with your goals. I think being open to the opportunity to help is invaluable. Analysts, teammates, partners, employees, teachers, doctors, or service providers are somewhere out there, waiting to be asked for help. Just be self-aware of shortcomings, and if you may need a hand to make your dreams and goals a reality.

While you are working on your self-awareness, be familiar with one pitfall that is easy to fall into… comparison. You could have all your goals and plans organized to perfection building up yourself in a capable, sensible, and relaxed manner. Then you run across someone you perceive as more successful, more sophisticated, and doing way more than you. The comparison scramble and pity party can begin. Spiraling you out of alignment, and placing you right into that risky decision zone. It happens. Just be aware of it, and progress accordingly. It may be time to adjust, pivot or recenter yourself.

Working on creating healthy environments in your personal and professional life is worthwhile. Try not to create environments where it's easy to let important issues go ignored to get through the day. It is important to be approachable with others' feelings, as well as your own. Take responsibility when problems are your fault and give apologies at every opportunity. Ask for help if you need to figure out how to change for the better. It is common to overlook your own mistakes. Sometimes, you are the person that needs to change, and it's hard to solve problems when you are in the same mind-frame that the problem was created with. That is not to say keeping toxic relationships in your life is necessary, by any means. Remove toxic relationships from your environment with a loving heart at the pace that works for you.

Self-awareness about your environment or living space being organized for maximum performance is a constructive element to becoming who you are. Some might say that it is a luxury to be able to live in the space of your dreams, embracing your own personal style, and I would probably agree. However, it is not impossible to start somewhere. Clean your desk.

Throw out old things that are worn out, do not fit anymore, or impede self-improvement. Make a collage of a dream wardrobe you plan to have when you have the money. Grab a pen or a laptop to start designing the complex elements of your universe in the way that works for you. There are many ways to start imagining your dream spaces.

There is probably going to be one person (or a hundred) in your life that might try to verbally squash your dreams. I always laugh when people say "You are a dreamer" as an insult. Usually they intend for that phrase to be a kind slap in the face, as if to say, "Snap out of it! Come back to the reality of what is possible in this world. You are dreaming if you think 'that' is going to happen." It is hilarious to me. I mean what is so awful about being a dreamer? What would be the contrary position to take? Stop going after your dreams. The road ends here. Just stop annoying everybody with your troublesome efforts to make your hopes and dreams come true. Well, as they say, "haters gonna hate." Treat haters with compassion, they probably need it most of all. Find your bright side, and keep being more awesome everyday moving forward with your dreams. You've got your path to happiness to adventure through.

I am just throwing this in here in case it is valuable: one of my biggest pet peeves is when people say you are the average of the five people you hang out with most. The sentiment here is to not hang out with losers for fear that it will make you a loser too. Okay, sure, maybe that has some merit. Hanging out with people that are doing great things is wonderful, and associating with shady characters is probably not the wisest decision. However, dumping friends because they are not successful enough is not cool.

There are "unsuccessful" friends that bring tons of goodwill, harmony, wisdom and understanding. If someone is lovely to be around, should they be dropped because they are not successful enough? No. That would be crazy. Plus, who is to say that every person has to achieve certain things by a certain timeline to be considered successful? I have lots of friends that are completely opposite from me in many ways, and we have an amazing time together. I have wealthy friends, I have broke friends. I hang out with them all equally in all types of situations. I don't use any of my friends to get ahead in life, unless we partner together on a project or business to be mutually rewarding. True friendship is the most amazing thing in the world. Try not to add or drop friends based on preconceived notions of getting yourself ahead.

Kindness is an important element to positive thinking and self-awareness. Being kind or helping is not for accolades. It just feels good showing up to add value with zero expectations. That does not mean that you have to be perfect, or that you will never accidentally hurt someone's feelings. Just find all the moments, as many moments as possible, that you can make kindness a habit. Put the grocery cart back in the proper place after unpacking the groceries in the car. No matter how far the jaunt is, or how many other people have decided to haphazardly throw all the carts around the parking lot. Every single time, rain or shine. We have all seen the random carts scattered around a parking lot, seemingly because someone just did not want to walk a few more feet to properly put it away. Everyone knows it is someone's job to collect the shopping carts to put them back inside the store. It is kind to make that person's job a little easier. When everyone properly puts away the shopping carts in the correct return spot it feels as if collectively we are all working together as a little polite microcosm. I love taking my shopping cart to the correct place. It has become a habit to appreciate the moment when someone that I will never meet experiences an easier day, because I made a decision to be thoughtful.

There are tiny acts of kindness that can make the world more awesome in big ways for people. Try to live your kindness moments at every chance you get to. Becoming who you are is about being the best you that you can be, and also about helping those around you be the best they can be. Kindness is something you can do one hundred percent of the time. However, giving is something you do as you have time, energy and resources for it.

I try to give something to someone everyday. I do not give money, because that's not necessarily my superpower. I certainly wish money was my superpower, but my superpower is ideas. I have piles of ideas. There is an endless stream of ideas constantly popping into my brain. I cannot use them all. Usually ideas will pop in my head listening to videos, scrolling social media, or just out-and-about doing stuff. If I get an idea, and think it would be a great one for someone, I simply send it to them. They can take it or leave it. What if they like the idea, and it makes them millions? It is so much better than just sitting inside my mind wasting away if it can help some do something awesome.

Sometimes, I try to give skills like branding, illustration, production or marketing help to friends as they may need a little boost of help. I do not just give free services and walk away. I try to do a little mentoring along the way to share some knowledge they may not have yet. I do what I can to support them, and make sure they know how to hire someone like me, and what it may cost for when they are ready.

Keep in mind that you do not have to say "yes' to every favor someone asks of you. Especially when they are asking you for products or services that you are trying to build a business with. For example, if you are a yoga teacher, and people keep asking you for free yoga classes. They may think it does not actually cost you any money to teach a yoga class. They may think "What is one more extra person in your class going to hurt?" They may think you would obviously just love the exposure to teach yoga at their event. If you cannot afford to give away your time or products for free, find a way that is comfortable for you to say no.

Sometimes, moments happen when you give and give and realize you are being taken advantage of, or just being unacknowledged in general. At some point giving away products or services while you are building your repertoire is valuable. But, there will be a day when you must charge or else you are not being valuable to yourself. There will be a time to comfortably give. If that time is not now, just give kindness.

NOTES

15

Kindness is an important element to positive thinking. Being kind or helping is not for accolades. It just feels good showing up to add value with zero expectations. That does not mean that you have to be perfect, or that you will never accidentally hurt someone's feelings. Just find all the moments, as many moments as possible, that you can make kindness a habit. Put the grocery cart back in the proper place after unpacking the groceries in the car. No matter how far the jaunt is, or how many other people have decided to haphazardly throw all the carts around the parking lot. Every single time, rain or shine. We have all seen the random carts scattered around a parking lot, seemingly because someone just did not want to walk a few more feet to properly put it away. Everyone knows it is someone's job to collect the shopping carts to put them back inside the store. It is kind to make that person's job a little easier. When everyone properly puts away the shopping carts in the correct return spot it feels as if collectively we are all working together as a little polite microcosm. I love taking my shopping cart to the correct place. It has become a habit to appreciate the moment when someone that I will never meet experiences an easier day, because I made a decision to be thoughtful.

There are tiny acts of kindness that can make the world more awesome in big ways for people. Try to live your kindness moments at every chance you get to. Becoming who you are is about being the best you that you can be, and also about helping those around you be the best they can be. Kindness is something you can do one hundred percent of the time. However, giving is something you do as you have time, energy and resources for it.

I try to give something to someone everyday. I do not give money, because that's not necessarily my superpower. I certainly wish money was my superpower, but my superpower is ideas. I have piles of ideas. There is an endless stream of ideas constantly popping into my brain. I cannot use them all. Usually ideas will pop in my head listening to videos, scrolling social media, or just out-and-about doing stuff. If I get an idea, and think it would be a great one for someone, I simply send it to them. They can take it or leave it. What if they like the idea, and it makes them millions? It is so much better than just sitting inside my mind wasting away if it can help some do something awesome.

Sometimes, I try to give skills like branding, illustration, production or marketing help to friends as they may need a little boost of help. I do not just give free services and walk away. I try to do a little mentoring along the way to share some knowledge they may not have yet. I do what I can to support them, and make sure they know how to hire someone like me, and what it may cost for when they are ready.

Keep in mind that you do not have to say "yes' to every favor someone asks of you. Especially when they are asking you for stuff that you are trying to build a business with. For example, if you are a yoga teacher, and people keep asking you for free yoga classes. They may think it does not actually cost you any money to teach a yoga class. They may think, what is one more extra person in your class going to hurt?" They may think you would obviously just love the exposure to teach yoga at their event? Sometimes those moments happen when you give and give and realize you are being taken advantage of, or just being unacknowledged in general. At some point giving away products or services while you are building your repertoire is valuable. But, there will be a day when you must charge or else you are not being valuable to yourself. There will be a time to comfortably give. If that time is not now, just give kindness.

CHAPTER 16 | REVERSE ENGINEER YOUR GOALS

I reverse engineer my goals. I do this naturally. I am so glad I discovered the term to identify my bizarre tactic of doing things backwards. Let me explain, when I was in college I started a band with my best friend. I could barely play guitar, but the band had officially started in my mind. I made all the T-shirt designs. I designed all the posters. I made album covers for all our albums that would take decades to release, and named all the songs before they were even written. I even held real band practice without having all the members needed, and even booked a show with a month to prepare without having an official drummer, which we needed for the performance. I was more scared of not doing it than I was scared of looking like a fool in front of people. I had seen plenty of bands that sucked, and I was honored if at the very worst I could be one of them. All I wanted was to be in the game. The regret of not doing it overshadowed any fears. Yes, it probably was a weird process to attempt to achieve a goal. I was fully aware of that. Ultimately, we did find a drummer to play that show. In a month's time, we practiced, performed, and it all went fine. No one laughed at us. Eventually, I learned how to play guitar well. Every show we played was decent enough as we went through the process of learning how to play live shows, and every show was invigorating to experience. Our band eventually recorded an album, and played shows with lots of new friend's bands. I reversed engineered it. I started with the goal of what I wanted in my mind, and then figured out how to make it happen later. The end is a great place to start.

Reverse engineering is sort of a deep-dive into your own imagination for planning. You start with the end goal in mind, and then map out all the possibilities of how you can get there. That does not mean you will always get your way, but it is the blueprint of how to make it happen with the best information you currently have. I am definitely reverse engineering this book right now. Writing is probably my weakest skill in my giant toolbox of skills I possess, yet here I am writing sentences, paragraphs and chapters… we will see how the final outcome turns out!

We all have dreams we are afraid to just freaking start implementing. How can you stop avoiding goals, and get to the good part of becoming who you are? Who cares about the expectations of what is "acceptable" or what is considered "successful." Making millions of dollars or winning awards is amazing, but perhaps simply busking in a subway terminal for fifty bucks a day traveling the world is happiness. The simple happiness of doing what you want to do everyday can be success no one could truly argue with. Pick an end goal, start imagining, and scheme up a game plan to carry out. Just be open to how things might unfold when your plans are put into motion in the real world. Being open to how things evolve will leave room for greater possibilities to happen for you.

Since we are talking about reversing engineering goals, this could be a good time to talk about "gatekeepers." Record labels, publishing companies, film and television studios, and many other professional entities that exist which require a "yes" to be included in the industry are what I deem "gatekeepers." They are slowly losing their grip on the culture of creators. Bad news for them, but good news for the majority of humans. Major companies, smaller independent companies, and DIY creators can all be involved in the game. There are enough eyeballs, and there is enough revenue to go around. There is always room for more art. If you want to sell tickets to your own movie, you can do that now all on your own. Because of the internet, the entire world can play your game, watch your show, read your book, or listen to your music the instant you release it. Sure, if you want to be on a professional sports team, you're going to have to try out and be accepted. However, it seems that across the board in many industries, gatekeepers are losing their grip, and it is very exciting.

Try not to be your own gatekeeper. Do not stop yourself from making your thing, because you are afraid of making something substandard or poor quality. My philosophy is to just create, publish, and get experience. The first rendition of your thing is probably going to be crummy on some level. Sometimes you have to get entry-level creations out of your system to move onto a more professional level. I know when brainstorming for new ideas, you have to write down those bad ideas just to get them out of your system to make room for the more innovative and unique ideas to start flowing out of you. Do not be afraid to suck. Be grateful to suck. I've heard it said that "perfection is just procrastination in disguise." I can definitely see that being a possibility. What is so scary about failure if you genuinely tried your best? It actually seems more terrifying to fail, because you are convinced that you were not ready, and never even tried.

CHAPTER 17 | YOU'VE ALREADY MADE IT

The point of this book is not to tell you to ignore reality, stay positive under all circumstances, or just stop being poor already. I tragically look on the bright side of all situations. It is just my nature. I do not expect everyone to be like me. Rather, I would like to think of this book simply as a confidence builder and personal happiness cheerleader. The one thing that I feel passionate about is helping people realize they do not have to live in daily drudgery. They can have goals and implement plans to build dream lifestyles. I am extremely good at not doing anything that I do not want to do, but I certainly have not made my millions yet. I am still on my own journey of becoming the ultimate vision of who I want to be and achieve all the things I want to achieve. If I realize tomorrow "I have peaked. That is it. There is nothing more I am ever going to achieve," then I still have the skills that I have built up in my life to feel comfortable just doing whatever I want to do everyday. I can embrace that this is just me. Simply enjoy my interests, my friends, my family, and live life. I will boldly love myself today, even if I never change.

Sometimes we punish ourselves daily with negative self-talk when it is taking forever to meet our own goals and expectations. It is hard to believe that success takes so long sometimes. We think we must be losers, because things just should just be freaking achieved already. Patience is a virtue, but not always easy. Just push forward. Improving skills, gaining more knowledge, and enjoying yourself at your pace is nothing to be ashamed about. Be unashamed to talk about how genius you are. Wear your favorite clothes everyday just to feel amazing. Forgive yourself for any faults you consistently beat yourself up over, and keep working on you. Everyone can improve on something in their life, even if they appear to have everything in the world and zero imperfections.

Some people say, "fake it till you make it" or "act as if," but I think it's okay to look at yourself and love and appreciate your reality while still striving for more. Forgive yourself for not being flawless. The past is gone, and who cares if tomorrow is not perfect. Love yourself today. Fall asleep with the intention that you will do your best to make tomorrow amazing, or maybe just one day closer to amazing.

We can all look back and romanticize the past, but when you are living your reality, it is very hard to appreciate the hard times. For example, when you are living in a tiny crappy apartment while you are wishing to be living in something more luxurious, you might be missing out on having fun appreciating the time spent there. When you look into the rearview, it is much easier to understand the relationships and adventures you experienced to get to where you are today. Enjoy all the moments. You will outgrow the tiny crappy apartment. Even though you may not ever want to live there again, you can look back on those times with fondness. I heard someone say once that you are like a potted plant. You get placed in a tiny pot to start, and then you get rerooted and placed in the next pot size as you grow. If you are always just obsessing about the next pot size, it makes it more difficult to have fun inside the pot you are in now.

Once at a New Year's Eve party, after the countdown, I was hugging my goodbyes to all my friends. Then one friend excitedly said to me, "This is going to be your year!" Which is a totally normal thing to say to people when everyone is making new year's resolutions.

But, something struck me as I was driving away from that party. Wait a minute. Does she think I'm not successful? Does she think I haven't "made it?" How does she know if last year wasn't my year? What if I just had the best year of my dreams, and I didn't broadcast it all over social media to be ogled over? I didn't, but what if I did? Rather than spiraling into the emotions that no one thinks I am successful. I had a big thought pop into my head! Like a big download from a mainframe. "I've already made it" snapped into my brain.

I have done a substantial amount of cool things. Not everything, but quite a bit of achievements. I'm just living the moments as they unfold. It feels like watching a movie that is already made, but also simultaneously being written, filmed, and edited. It's up to me how boring this movie is. I think maybe we all have already made it. It is just hard to see sometimes, because we are right in the middle of the movie. Have fun making it.

I know this sounds like the ramblings of a crazy lady, but maybe you have already made it, too. Whatever your goals are, give yourself permission to execute your plans, and just be proud of yourself today. An unconventional idea only seems crazy and weird until one day it is epic. Enjoy the process, and watch it unfold.

This is not a financial book. I encourage you to go find your own money gurus that you love and connect with their methodology and advice. It has been said that there are a million ways to make money, and a billion ways to lose money. I cannot give financial advice. The more I learn, try, succeed and fail, the more I have come to believe that financial security is inside my brain. This is just my experience of how lifestyle freedom works for me.

Lifestyle freedom does not mean retirement. It does not mean working just one hour a day, or working from a laptop from a beach cabana. For me, it means earmarking everyday for working on the projects I want to work on for as long as I am blessed with the ability to think and create. It is about figuring out the best revenue streams for you to build your own unique career. A salary could be a revenue stream. Being an independent contractor with clients could be a revenue stream. Royalties from books or albums sales could be a revenue stream. Advertising compensation, interests, dividends, rental income or sales could all be ways to earn income. It is just a puzzle that you need to solve for yourself. Sure, the term "financial freedom" sounds nice, but I do not think your brain ever stops working on how to experience more, be a lifelong learner, and continually improve yourself. Most of us go through the natural process of learning how to pay the bills every month. Then, we move to working in order to have the nice things we always wanted and to be comfortable. Next, we may start preparing to know how to invest for the future when we cannot physically do as much. Then we kick ourselves for buying nice things when we are young and not starting to invest sooner, but that's how the cookie crumbles.

When designing your lifestyle freedom, it is all about positioning yourself to make money doing the things you want to do, and learning how to scale those revenue streams at a comfortable pace. Once you have talent, skills, and education, you can probably confidently make money at a professional level. It can feel like true freedom, but there are a few things to think about as you are becoming successful. Making money is not the endgame for every goal. While working on skills and building up dream streams, why not also think about scaling your efforts. Scaling is something that happens later in your journey, and it will not work for every situation. Three things I often think about is, how I can create evergreen products where I spend time making a product once to sell over and over again? What will it look like to scale production levels to sell and ship 100,000 units? If I need a change and want to sell a successful revenue stream, what is that process? I have heard it said that running a 5-star hotel is actually easier than running a 2-star hotel. How will you invest your time? Is there a shift in the way you are doing things that could make your output easier and more luxurious? What is the exit strategy, if needed?

Building wealth and making money is not a one-size-fits-all situation. The solution for you is as unique as your DNA. I bet even the richest billionaire in the world has questions and problems they need to figure out all the time. Even billionaires ask for help. Teaching yourself how to pay all the bills for a lifetime can be a pain. Food, clothing, shelter, water, electricity, internet, phone and transportation, is a necessity for most in general. Not to mention, lifestyle inflation is hard to avoid. Lifestyle inflation is where we spend more money when we don't need to, just because we are making more money. Being sensible and wise with money is fundamental, but thinking small and being cheap can hold us back as well. It feels like a constant balancing act between making prudent financial decisions and taking risks to level-up.

If you are curious, my method is to get my basic living expenses as low as humanly possible. I keep the allotment of funds for my living expenses to be one of three accounts that I have financially planned for. Like most people, this account is my most important account to fund. I try to keep it as full as I possibly can. Some people consider that to be an emergency fund. It is a fund of several months or so of cash expenses saved to be spent in case unexpectedly there is no money coming in, and you need to cover your bills without a hiccup. Having several months of living expenses saved up was not something I did when I held a salary position. When I had a secure paycheck coming in every month, I barely saved. When I did save for something, it was only to buy extras, or go on vacations with friends. I learned to have an emergency fund when I became a freelancer. Working as a digital nomad had its fringe benefits, but consistent paychecks was not one of them. Like clockwork, I always made the exact money I needed to make every month working on gigs. However when you are a freelancer, you always know there is a chance that the next job might not come through. You always need a backup plan. The habit of accumulating huge chunks of monthly living expense savings is not as impossible as it seems when you frame it in your mind differently. Having months or years of living expenses managed and saved up is flexibility, calmness, and freedom to make more choices. For me, that is way more exciting than spending money on extras. Every time a living expense bill finds my eyeballs, I feel proud and so grateful that I can pay this bill with ease. Always remember that anything can happen to put anyone back in the stressful mindset of feeling panic for not having money for bills. It brings me peace and mental spending balance to get excited to save money for bills.

Once I have a very comfortable amount of time saved for the basic living expenses, the wealth created beyond that will go into two different buckets. I have an account for extras, and an account to build up investments. It is healthy to go out to dinner sometimes, and spend a little extra on yourself. Meeting friends for drinks, upgrading a vehicle, or buying new clothes and decor are all extraneous purchases. I celebrate splurge purchases differently than I celebrate paying for basic living costs. I am improving on my cheap mindest the older I get. Saving all the time can be a little daunting, so I work on spending without guilt and try to dream a little bigger when it comes to extras. There is a balance there between growing healthy spending expectations and sensible money management.

The third bank account I am trying to build is my investments account. Maybe there are fourth and fifth financial accounts needed for more levels of wealth once you start achieving more. I'm not sure. What I do know is that it's possible to teach yourself the process that works for you while designing your own lifestyle freedom.

Another little tip is to organize and prepare your ideal budget, even if you do not have any money. Don't pray for money. Prepare for money. Journal about what you would do with a million dollars. Interview others about what they would do with a million dollars to make it grow? Another interesting question would be to ask people what would they do if they had zero dollars in their bank account today? How would they rebuild themselves back up? Money seems to be attracted to and flows towards where it is understood and treated well. Your financial education and implementation skills will be your greatest tools to help you succeed with money. Think of money as your favorite best friend who you want to be around all the time. Money brings your energy up, and can help you be the best you can be. Like a good friendship, if you want more time with them, you have to work at it. You have to make time for money, and bring value to money for it to stick around.

Even in a bad economy, prosperity growth can actually happen. Let me explain. When I quit my salary position as an Art Director of a record label in Los Angeles to be an independent contractor, it was perfect timing. I did not plan to make such a speculative career move smack in the middle of the financial crisis of 2007-2008. I had a little money saved, and only one plan, to hopefully get clients. Things were going great for me at the time, and the crash had little effect on me personally. Did the financial crisis end up destroying my plans? On the contrary, it just happened to make my life as a freelance designer a little easier. I exclusively worked on music design, because that was my interest. That was before "picking a niche" was a thing.

Just in case this is randomly helpful knowledge for someone, I have to throw in this tangential thought for freelancers: Being available to every possible client in the world is nice, but focusing and narrowing your offerings to one type of client makes your life so much easier in some biarrare way. For example, a web designer who only builds sites for doctors and dentists, a filmmaker who only gets hired to make skydiving memorabilia videos, a photographer who only takes photos of pets, or an interior designer who only designs commercial spaces. Sure, an expert is capable of doing all sorts of different projects, and accepting jobs outside of a niche is totally fine. However, pigeonholing yourself down and marketing your skills to a specific industry style is an instant selling point for your service. It feels easier for people to recommend your business to others that need your distinctive service. It also helps with fine-tuning your own marketing efforts; and pitching yourself to potential clients.

So, back to the story. I had my niche, and a variety of services that I would do for musicians and record labels. With a few months of successful contracted gigs completed under my belt, it started to become obvious that a financial crash was hitting Los Angeles. Tons of layoffs were happening, and record labels were downsizing their art departments left and right. The labels still needed design work to be done, but they could not seem to afford a thoroughly staffed art department of full-time employees. Luckily for me, I wasn't looking for a job, I was looking for clients. It was perfect timing. Magically, all at once, I was getting comfortable with the process of being a hired gun, and labels were outsourcing talent. It was a perfect match. I am not sure what I would have done if I had been one of those thousands of people suddenly let go from a downsizing company. Auspiciously, my freelance experiment was well-timed.

I was having a blast working from a laptop. I found myself making the same amount of money finding my own gigs, as working a steady office salary position. I was learning about business, money, and taxes. I was cutting frivolous expenses at every turn. Learning this process was essential for me learning how to develop my lifestyle freedom. I never wanted to be the best graphic designer in the world, so I moved on from doing client work to learn something new. I am still on the search for learning more ways I personally can create revenue streams without clients. However, that skill is always in my back pocket if I ever need to use it.

Many people have lost fortunes multiple times, and they get back up and try again. Some people want to live a simple slow living existence. Some people love the hustle with every minute of every day scheduled with something to do. Most people lie somewhere in between working at a super relaxed pace, and having thrilling go-getter moments. Carefully, make some magical career decisions for yourself. Try your ideas. Test stuff out. Broaden your skills, experiences and accomplishments. When becoming who you are, think about the work being the reward, and the money is just the result. Design your day for personal fulfillment. Nothing in life is guaranteed. Do your best!

Wouldn't it be nice if you could inspire just one person? Whatever it is that you have decided to put out in the world, there is one person noticing and being inspired by it. That person is you, inspire yourself.

Even if you think you are not perfect or are afraid people will instantly cringe when they see what you are trying to do, we all have to start somewhere. If no one else is really watching, did it even happen? Who cares what they think. They do not have to live your life. Inspire yourself to do all the things you want to do.

You have artistic freedom. No one needs to give you permission to do the things you want to do. I know it is painful sometimes to think you might suck, but no one needs to think you are cool. That is not a requirement to experience things, and create the life you want.

People will hate it. People will ignore it. Try to free yourself from opinions, and have fun. What if there is one person out there watching what you are doing, and feeling activated, energized and motivated to try what you are trying? That is an incredible energy exchange humans are supposed to be experiencing. Do not die with your art inside you. Embrace your weirdness, and try your best to express yourself in your own unique way. Free yourself from trying to keep up with algorithms to be popular, or other people's timelines and standards. Love yourself today, and change only to impress yourself.

If along your way, you are lucky enough to find someone that inspires you who will mentor you in some fashion, that is amazing. For most people, it is just not something that happens to all. Working under someone is a great mentorship experience to see how the wheels of a machine really work. If it is available to you, seeing how a successful business works from the inside is an unparalleled experience. I would never turn down the opportunity to learn something I need to learn while working under someone else if it is possible. They take the risk, and you take the knowledge. Brilliant.

Paying for professional advice can really give you a head start as well. But most of us cannot be frivolous with time or money. So, what are some alternatives to paying for help or finding a cool apprenticeship at the perfect time? I guess we sort of just get left with mentoring ourselves. The internet and your local library is a major resource. Taking local community college classes can help those in-person learners sometimes at a reasonable rate. There are online courses. I would stay away from those overpriced courses on how to build courses, or courses that promise to teach you something that would be physically humanly impossible to teach online for $997 dollars.

It is true that the online education space is a billion dollar industry. Some courses out there must be helpful. I would just be very careful with how much you are willing to spend, or lose, on courses that may not actually deliver on the sales pitch they sold you on to sign up.

This warning also goes for online coaches and expensive mastermind groups. These things do exist. I am sure there are people out there that have obtained tons of value from them, but I do not personally know one. However, there are people out there with the absolute opposite opinion, and believe expensive coaches and courses are how you take things to the next-level of success. There are people that think you cannot possibly learn everything you need to learn by watching free video tutorials. I have learned so much from the online tutorial space for tech advice, business tips and personal hacks. I know there is value in free online education. I can see how paying for someone to give you a headstart could be helpful. Time is money, but educating yourself as much as possible on a topic before you invest seems wise.

Just be aware that you can lose money when investing in education. There are people out there that regret their entire college degree that came with a six-figure price tag. I have invested a very small amount of money into online courses, and it was more for educational entertainment over promises that it would change my life. When I purchased a course, I was financially secure and perfectly fine with losing the money if the course was not necessarily valuable. In fact, now that I think about it, I used Christmas and birthday gift money to purchase those courses, so that I would not feel as bad if they sucked. I did not spend my last two hundred bucks or go into debt trying to find solutions to problems. Just my two cents warning on that. I only mentioned this, because there is a conversation happening right now around this issue. There are people out there right now predatorily selling products you do not need to succeed, and begging others to sign up for multi-level marketing companies that turn out to be pyramid schemes.

Try not to fall into guru traps. Try not to be manipulated into buying something before you are ready. False scarcity exists. People can prey on your lack and sadness. Those countdown clocks on a sales page to "buy now before it's too late" are manipulating you. Also, sometimes when you miss out on purchasing something for whatever reason, you tend to get over it very quickly and even sometimes forget you even ever wanted it. If you cannot stop thinking about something you want to buy, maybe it actually is something that resonates with you soul, and you should go back to figure out how to buy it when you are ready. Use your intuition.

Being the architect of your life is all about your personal power and your intuition. Your feelings are your goals. Your confidence will build your achievements. Security is the knowledge inside you. Take your best shot at all the ideas in your head you want to attempt. Design your path. Communicate the personal brand of you by broadcasting your essence, and then monetizing yourself. I'm becoming who I am in front of you right now. I would love to see the entire world do it too. Now go, and become who you are.

NOTES

1. Pick five of your favorite songs you would like to play.

2. Find someone to teach you how to play those songs in order from easy to most difficult.

3. Once you hear yourself playing one song that you love, find a friend to practice with weekly.

4. Book a show anywhere before you feel ready to perform in public.

5. Play the show

6. Repeat process to not suck, and get better at playing

Guitar playing goal achieved!
No one cares if your show is terrible if you are having fun on stage.

THANK *you*
for hanging out with me

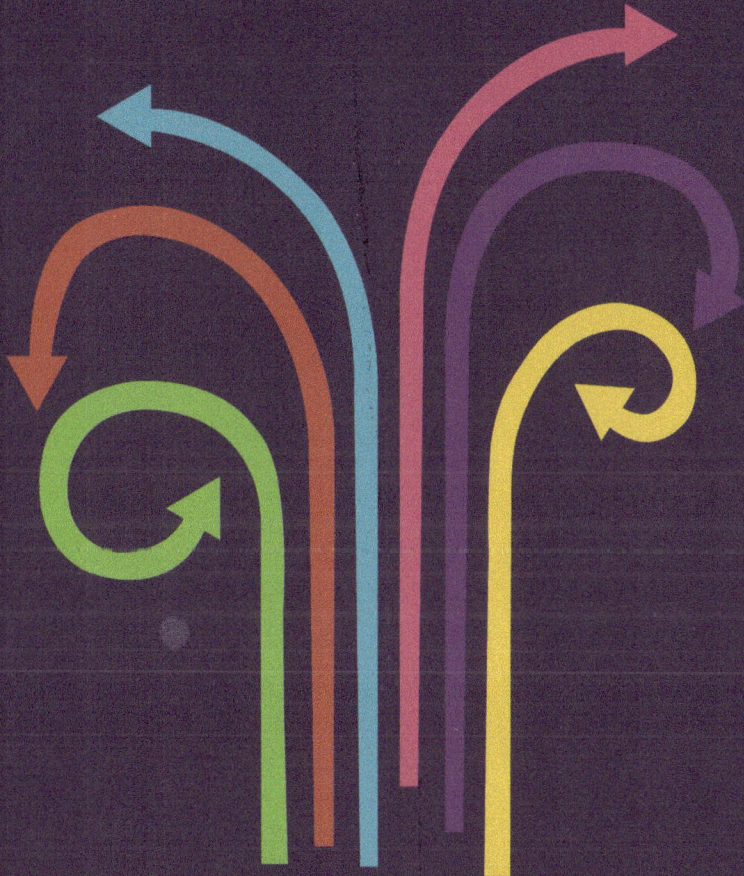

check OUT more BOOKS

TITLE:
Goal Morning Workbook
ISBN:
978-1-954557-05-5

TITLE:
Goal Night Workbook
ISBN:
978-1-954557-06-2

TITLE:
Personal Brand Diary
ISBN:
978-1-954557-13-0

TITLE:
Idea Diary
ISBN:
978-1-954557-11-6

TITLE:
Mini Manifest Diary
ISBN:
978-1-954557-14-7

TITLE:
Mini Idea Diary
ISBN:
978-1-954557-10-9

www.ingramcontent.com/pod-product-compliance
Lightning Source LLC
Chambersburg PA
CBHW062022050526
44107CB00106B/938